Francia
Ingilterra
Svezia
Danimarca
Russia
Polonia
Ragusa
Malta
Curlandia   Luneburgo   Brema   Genova   Pontefice
Stati uniti di America
Algeri   Marrocco   China   Giappone   Mogol   Persia

7. Band.ᵃ d'Ammiraglio
8. Band. della Com.ᵃ dell'Indie
9. Detta di Scozia
   Spagna

Napoli
1. Band. di Guer.ᵃ e Mercan.
2. Altra detta Mercantile
   Svezia

Sardegna
1. Band. di Guer.ᵃ e Mercantile
2. Particolare Sarda
   Prussia

Band.ᵃ Mercantile
Polonia
Band. di Guer.ᵃ e Mercantile
Olanda

Malta
Band. di Guer.ᵃ e Mercantile
2. Detta di Gr.
Mastro

THE ITALIANS
AND THE CREATION
OF AMERICA

THE ITALIANS AND THE CREATION OF AMERICA

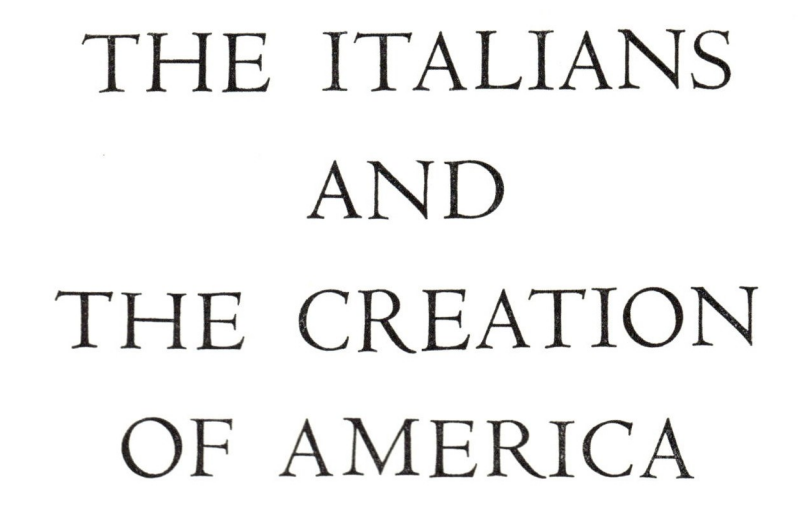

An Exhibition at the

John Carter Brown Library

Brown University

prepared by

Samuel J. Hough

PROVIDENCE · RHODE ISLAND · 1980

Endpapers: Vincenzo Scotti. Tavole delle . . . bandiere. Leghorn, 1796. 49×39 cm. Cat. no. 127.

© COPYRIGHT 1980 BY BROWN UNIVERSITY
LIBRARY OF CONGRESS CATALOGUE NUMBER 80-81557

Contents

Foreword BY VINCENT J. BUONANNO *page 7*

Patrons 9

Preface BY THOMAS R. ADAMS 11

Introduction BY SAMUEL J. HOUGH 13

List of Plates 17

Abbreviations of Works Cited Most Frequently 19

I The Discovery of Discovery (*catalogue numbers* 1–5) 23
II Columbus (6–10) 26
III Vespucci (11–17) 29
IV The Impact of the Discoveries upon Italy (18–25) 32
V Italian Historians of the Great Explorations (26–36) 37
VI The Reputation of Columbus in Italy (37–45) 42
VII Vespucci as a Theme in Cinquecento Italian Poetry (46–48) 45
VIII Italian Physicians and America (49–52) 47
IX Italian Missionaries on the Frontiers of Seventeenth-Century America (53–56) 49
X The Seventeenth Century (57–62) 51
XI Italian Erudition and the Preservation of American Artifacts (63–66) 53
XII Italian Influence on the Arts in Colonial America (67–69) 55
XIII Jesuits from America Exiled to Italy (70–72) 56
XIV Italian Awareness of English America, 1750–1775 (73–81) 58
XV Benjamin Franklin and the Italians (82–87) 61
XVI Italian Contributions to American Political Thought (88–90) 64
XVII Italians and the American Revolution (91–97) 65
XVIII The Italian Cartographic Tradition (98–127) 68

Index 81

THE ITALIANS
AND
THE CREATION
OF AMERICA

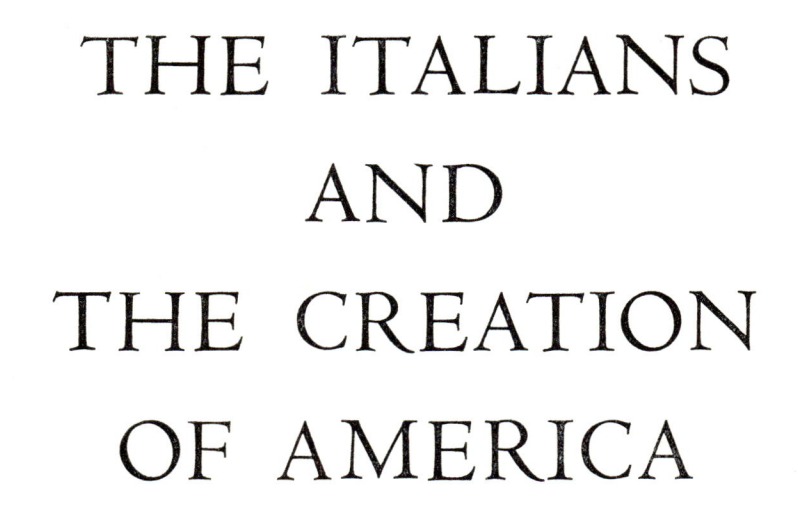

An Exhibition at the

John Carter Brown Library

Brown University

prepared by

Samuel J. Hough

PROVIDENCE · RHODE ISLAND · 1980

Endpapers: Vincenzo Scotti. Tavole delle . . . bandiere. Leghorn, 1796. 49×39 cm. Cat. no. 127.

© COPYRIGHT 1980 BY BROWN UNIVERSITY
LIBRARY OF CONGRESS CATALOGUE NUMBER 80-81557

Contents

Foreword BY VINCENT J. BUONANNO *page 7*

Patrons 9

Preface BY THOMAS R. ADAMS 11

Introduction BY SAMUEL J. HOUGH 13

List of Plates 17

Abbreviations of Works Cited Most Frequently 19

I The Discovery of Discovery (*catalogue numbers 1–5*) 23

II Columbus (6–10) 26

III Vespucci (11–17) 29

IV The Impact of the Discoveries upon Italy (18–25) 32

V Italian Historians of the Great Explorations (26–36) 37

VI The Reputation of Columbus in Italy (37–45) 42

VII Vespucci as a Theme in Cinquecento Italian Poetry (46–48) 45

VIII Italian Physicians and America (49–52) 47

IX Italian Missionaries on the Frontiers of Seventeenth-Century America (53–56) 49

X The Seventeenth Century (57–62) 51

XI Italian Erudition and the Preservation of American Artifacts (63–66) 53

XII Italian Influence on the Arts in Colonial America (67–69) 55

XIII Jesuits from America Exiled to Italy (70–72) 56

XIV Italian Awareness of English America, 1750–1775 (73–81) 58

XV Benjamin Franklin and the Italians (82–87) 61

XVI Italian Contributions to American Political Thought (88–90) 64

XVII Italians and the American Revolution (91–97) 65

XVIII The Italian Cartographic Tradition (98–127) 68

Index 81

FOREWORD

THE catalogue of "The Italians and the Creation of America" may seem a rather late arrival for a 1976 exhibition, but it may also be looked at as the very earliest of the forthcoming 1992 observances of the five-century-old relationship between the Italians and the New World. Unorthodox viewpoints aside, there is surely no other place in our country and probably not in the world where the first three centuries of this five-hundred-year link could be more richly documented than at the John Carter Brown Library. In the invaluable books, maps, and prints described in this volume the story is told of Italian participation in the great adventure of early America.

The selection of books described in these pages includes acquisitions of Mr. John Carter Brown made as early as 1846, and others made by the Library as late as 1979. "The Italians and the Creation of America" is, then, an idea still in the making, with origins in a private family collection which could never again be gathered; its future integrity and growth are assured as an institutional collection. The Library's treasures have played a prominent role in illuminating the first centuries of American history. This catalogue and the more extensive cataloguing activity under the leadership of Thomas Adams should make the Library's future even brighter.

The exhibition of this volume's contents in 1976 and 1977 proved most stimulating even to the public at large. This seems remarkable when one considers the barrier of language. There are several ways in which the collection overcomes this barrier. The sheer depth of original source materials extends from Marco Polo, in the late thirteenth century, through Carlo Botta, an important figure in the movement for Italian independence in the early nineteenth century. The collection traces the rebirth of the science of geography in the Renaissance; the voyages of the great Italian explorers; and the role of the Italian cartographers whose maps show us a combination of hard-won knowledge and entrepreneurial optimism. We also see the work of Italian printers, who produced the largest number of books about America in the sixteenth century, and the writings of Italian economists and philosophers, who were among the first Europeans to understand the potential of wealth and political unrest in the New World. One can also enjoy the collection purely for its visual delights—the examples of beautiful bookmaking, the superb draftsmanship of all the maps—in particular the Agnese Atlas, an exquisite four-hundred-year-old evidence of that Italian need to embellish the functional.

The catalogue of the exhibition "The Italians and the Creation of America" is the result of the labors and the generosity of many people. Most notable is Samuel Hough, assistant librarian of the John Carter Brown Library, who dreamed of this volume's realization, enkindled the interest and involvement of its patrons, then assembled the exhibition and wrote the catalogue. The members of the fundraising committee were Joseph Muratore, Armand Versaci, Anthony Mastronardi, James Twaddell, Ronald Del-Sesto, Angelo DiMario, Guy Settipane, Eugene Russo, and Brown University students Gianmaria Delzanno and Antonio Lorenzotti. It was through the diligence and goodwill of this committee that we have a group of men and women, mostly of Rhode Island, who are the book's patrons and are responsible entirely for its funding.

Vincent J. Buonanno

PATRONS

Mr. Robert M. Andreoli
Mr. & Mrs. Vincent J. Buonanno
Mr. & Mrs. George E. Conley
Mr. & Mrs. Ugo Gasbarro
Comm. & Mrs. Joseph R. Muratore
Mr. & Mrs. Alfred J. Petteruti
Dr. & Mrs. Eugene Russo
Dr. & Mrs. Guy Settipane
Joseph S. Sinclair Family Trust
Mr. & Mrs. Tempel Smith

Columbus National Bank
Grand Lodge of Rhode Island Order of the Sons of Italy in America
Rhode Island Hospital Trust National Bank

Mr. Louis Agnes
Miss Irma Antenucci
Mr. & Mrs. Adolf Buonanno
Mr. & Mrs. Bernard V. Buonanno, Sr.
Mr. & Mrs. Joseph E. Buonanno
Mr. & Mrs. Maury Caito
Mr. & Mrs. Thomas J. Caldarone
Mr. & Mrs. Edward F. Capaldi
Mr. & Mrs. Edmund F. Capozzi
Mr. & Mrs. Vito Carneglia
Dr. & Mrs. Francis H. Chafee

Dr. & Mrs. William P. Corvese
Mr. & Mrs. Ronald W. DelSesto
Mr. Robert A. di Curcio
Mr. & Mrs. Angelo DiMario
Mr. & Mrs. Thomas P. Dimeo
Mr. & Mrs. Edward DiSano
Mr. & Mrs. Peter Farago
Mr. Joseph R. Fazzano
Mr. & Mrs. Louis Fazzano
Mr. Conrad Ferla
Mr. & Mrs. Roland Fiore

Dr. & Mrs. Victor Formisano
Mr. Michael A. Gammino
Mr. & Mrs. Lombard J. Gasbarro
Mr. & Mrs. Thomas G. Gattone
Mr. John J. Giacchi
Mr. & Mrs. William H. D. Goddard
Dr. & Mrs. Thomas J. Howell
Mr. & Mrs. Henry Ise
Mr. & Mrs. Dan Lancellotti
Mr. & Mrs. William F. Leonelli
Mr. Frederick Lippitt
Mr. Royal Little
Mr. & Mrs. Biagio Maggiacomo
Mr. Allison J. Maggiolo
Mr. Walter A. Maggiolo
Mr. & Mrs. Mark P. Malkovich III
Mr. & Mrs. A. Mammoliti
Mr. Anthony Mansolillo
Mr. Vincent Marino
Miss Rose Mastrati
Mr. & Mrs. Anthony D. Mastronardi
Mr. & Mrs. Edmund M. Mauro, Jr.
Mr. Albert Medici
Dr. & Mrs. Frank Merlino
Dr. & Mrs. Peter J. Mogayzel
Mr. & Mrs. Ernest Nathan
Mr. & Mrs. John Parolisi
Mr. & Mrs. John O. Pastore
Mr. Umberto Patalano
Judge & Mrs. Raymond J. Pettine

Mr. & Mrs. N. Everett Picchione
Mr. & Mrs. Ronald R. S. Picerne
Mr. & Mrs. Felix A. Porcaro
Judge Vincent Ragosta
Mr. & Mrs. Edward W. Ricci
Mr. & Mrs. Joseph G. Samartano
Mr. & Mrs. Alfred J. Sammartino
Mr. & Mrs. Pasco Sammartino
Dr. & Mrs. A. A. Savastano
Mr. & Mrs. Vincent T. Sciotti
Dr. & Mrs. Fiorindo A. Simeone
Dr. & Mrs. Louis V. Sorrentino
Mr. Bruce Sundlun
Dr. & Mrs. Alfred Toselli
Mr. & Mrs. James F. Twaddell
Mr. Fred Ulbrich
Dr. & Mrs. Armand D. Versaci
Mr. & Mrs. Anthony Viola
Mr. & Mrs. John C. A. Watkins
Mr. & Mrs. Peter P. Zavota
Dr. & Mrs. Vincent Zecchino
Mrs. Celeste Feci Zucconi
Mr. David J. Zucconi

Cardi Corporation
Citizen's Bank
The Italian Echo
Textron
Unitam

PREFACE

ITALY played a leading role in the forces of the Renaissance that broke down the fixed and circumscribed world known to Europe at the beginning of the fifteenth century and opened it for the acceptance of new ideas and new experiences. Major among those new experiences was the discovery of the New World. Primary figures in this achievement were Italians: Cristoforo Colombo and Giovanni Caboto of Genova demonstrated that there were lands beyond the western ocean which were within reach of sailors bold enough to venture into the unknown; Amerigo Vespucci and Giovanni da Verrazzano of Firenze delineated the broad outlines of the eastern coasts of the American continents; Antonio Pigafetta of Vicenza set down the first-hand account of Magellan's voyage that placed the two new continents in their proper place on the map of the world while Pietro d'Anghiera of Arona on Lago Maggiore became the official chroniclers of New Spain.

Earlier Europeans had visited islands and lands in the Atlantic, but they neither understood the significance of what they saw nor were able to communicate the news of what they found to the rest of Europe. As more and more information about lands and peoples unknown to the Scriptures or to the ancients flowed back through Portugal and Spain, it was the ecclesiastical humanistic scholars of Italy who absorbed it, relating it to what was known and interpreting its meaning. The printing press had been in Italy only thirty years when Colombo returned, and it was through it that the significance of what was happening reached the rest of Europe. Likewise it was the Italian cartographers who began the redrawing of maps to accommodate the physical reality of a fourth part of the world.

The exhibition, of which this catalogue is a permanent record, treats both the leading place occupied by the Italians in the opening years of the history of the Americas and the part they continued to play in the process of exploration and settlement. Not only did individual Italians occupy a prominent part in the important work of the colonizing nations, Spain, Portugal, France, and England, but they were an important element of the larger task of the Church of bringing Christianity to the peoples of America. Out of all this activity grew a substantial body of writing by Italians about America which deserves attention in its own right.

For almost one hundred and fifty years the John Carter Brown Library has been assembling the printed record in which is revealed, in all of its ramifications, what happened during the three centuries following what Francisco de Gómara described in 1552 as "the greatest event since the creation of the world, excepting the incarnation and death of Him who created it ... the discovery of the Indies." In the process of creating this great collection new points of view and new insights are revealed to help the continuing process of understanding what happened to the Old World as a result of the discovery of the New. The Library welcomes this opportunity to draw upon its resources to illuminate the important part played by Italians in that process.

The exhibition was opened on December 9th, 1976, as a contribution to the Bicentennial celebrations. On that occasion we were honored by the presence of His Excellency Roberto Gaja, Ambassador of the Republic of Italy to the United States, and the Consul General of Italy at Boston, Franco Faa' di Bruno.

The inception and execution of both the exhibition and this catalogue were primarily the work of Mr. Vincent Buonanno, the Chairman of the Committee, and Mr. Samuel Hough, the Assistant Librarian of the John Carter Brown Library. Without the support of the patrons who contributed toward its publication, this catalogue could not have taken the form which it has. The Library is grateful to all these people who have so generously supported this endeavour.

Thomas R. Adams
Librarian

INTRODUCTION

THE contributions of Italians to the creation of America began well before the voyages of Columbus. Italian merchants had traveled throughout the known world for centuries. Some of them ventured into areas unknown to all but a very few Europeans, and their reports, reflecting the mercantile virtues of keen observation, bold curiosity, and self-possession in the face of adversity and in the midst of alien surroundings, expanded the geographical knowledge of all Europe and raised questions about what lay beyond the horizon. Then, in 1406, the cultural fruit of Italian mercantile activity—the movement we call the Renaissance—introduced a new element to geographical thought: the classical, theoretical geography of the second-century author Claudius Ptolemy. The recovery of Ptolemaic texts made possible by a Florentine merchant, Palla Strozzi, provided a structure for the detailed information being sent back from distant lands. Ptolemy's *Geography* excited curiosity for further information and enabled readers to relate that information to an expandable framework while at the same time questioning the limits of that framework. Thus, while the Venetian Cà da Mosto, who sailed for Prince Henry in the 1450's, shared many characteristics of Marco Polo, Cà da Mosto wrote, and was read, in a very different context. Marco Polo's China had seemed a strange, fantastic land unconnected with the world of Polo's audience. The sub-Saharan Africa described by Cà da Mosto was an extension of the world: a piece to fit into an incomplete puzzle. Observation interpreted by theory and theory tested by observation make the interplay required by scientific discovery. And within two distinct but related Italian traditions that interplay existed and resulted in nearly a century of creative geographical thinking that preceded, and resulted in, Columbus's discovery.

The great Italian explorers—Columbus, the Cabots, Vespucci, Verrazzano—all came from Italian merchant colonies abroad. They were *Italiani fuori d'Italia*, Italians outside of Italy. They shared the culture and the values of those colonies and shared a centuries-old tradition of Italians serving as the intellectuals of Europe—as financiers, architects, advisors, teachers, engineers, and explorers to every court of the continent. While loyal to the service of their masters—the Kings of Spain, England, Portugal, and France—Italians abroad never lost their *Italianità*, reinforced perhaps by their being *fuori d'Italia*.

Perhaps the most important contributions of the Italian explorers were intellectual. Surely, they risked their lives. But even more than the physical risks taken, they conceived bold, well-founded plans, made accurate and intelligent assessments, and reported in clear and vivid language. It was these characteristics which made the contributions of Italian explorers out of proportion to the number of individuals involved—characteristics which Italians had practiced in their own affairs and in service to foreign rulers for several centuries.

The most graphic expression of this Italian tradition was in their mapmaking. Italian experience at sea had been combined with the ability to resolve the mathematics of navigation to create an Italian school of mapmaking which was centuries old by the time of Columbus. The practical need of the merchant traveler to find his way at sea was expressed in beautiful portolan charts which were precise and, for those trained to use them, scientific. The Age of Discovery taxed Italian cartographers. Information about new lands arrived from second-hand sources and was often imprecise, perhaps garbled, and frequently conflicted with other information. The cartographer had to incorporate the information while resolving the more complex mathematical formulas required to portray a world expanding with each decade. The boldness of Italian cartographers in confronting these problems, the skill, imagination, and patience required for such confrontation, is not as well recognized as the comparable achievements of the explorers. Yet the cartographers of Genoa, Venice, and Rome helped to create the way America was perceived and understood.

The world map of 1569 by Giacomo Gastaldi represents a turning point in the role of Italian cartography and America, and in the role of Italian culture and America as well. In 1570 Abraham Ortelius in Antwerp started publishing a series of maps which signalled the shift of cartographic dominance to the cities of northwestern Europe. Diplomatic, economic, political, and to some degree cultural dominance was shifting concurrently from the Mediterranean to the Atlantic.

For the next two centuries, individual Italians participated in aspects of America, but America existed only on the fringes of Italian culture. The presence of Spain, both in America and Italy, prevented direct participation in America by any of the Italian city-states (there were early hopes in Tuscany to do so) and Italy did not greatly benefit from the expansion of wealth which the colonial powers shared.

The experience of the American Revolution returned America to a more important place in Italian culture. Benjamin Franklin played a symbolic role in representing America as a place where the ideals of the Enlightenment were realized. The example of the thirteen colonies, each retaining sovereign rights, uniting to solve common problems and freeing themselves from a foreign power, was admired by many Italians. Carlo Botta studied the American Revolution for its application to Italy; Vittorio Alfieri wrote odes praising its leaders; Carli, Maffei, Castiglioni studied the society which supported it.

One consequence of the absence of Italy as a colonial power in America is that the contributions of Italians in creating America have not received much attention. While this Exhibition can only touch upon certain aspects of those contributions, we hope to foster greater interest and further study of the subject.

The Exhibition is drawn entirely from the collections of the John Carter Brown Library. Many books were in the original collection formed by John Carter Brown between 1846 and 1874. Although the founder of the Library left statements concerning his concept of its goals, the breadth and richness of his collecting reveal his deep vision and the variety of his conception of the subject of America. Some of the finest individual items in this Exhibition, including the Agnese and Maggiolo atlases, the 1477 Ptolemy, and the illustrated Basel, 1493, edition of the Columbus letter, were added by John Carter Brown's son, John Nicholas Brown. When John Nicholas Brown died in 1900, his will left the "Bibliotheca Americana," money to construct a library building, and an endowment for its maintenance, to Brown University as a memorial to his father. Succeeding librarians, George Parker Winship, Worthington Chauncey Ford, Lawrence Counselman Wroth, and Thomas Randolph Adams, have enlarged and enriched the collection. Books added by each of them are found in the Exhibition. The collection of maps given to the Library by George H. Beans between 1957 and 1962 is especially commemorated in the text. When the Exhibition opened in December of 1976 we were able to say that "seven of the nine books in Case Four were obtained within the last two years, including the Venice, 1543, edition of Albergati's *La Pazzia* which arrived in the Library just three weeks before the opening of the Exhibition." Since that time other books have been obtained, and we have been able to include some of them in this catalogue.

The Exhibition rests upon a great foundation laid over a century ago, but much of its character and diversity reflect the active expansion and continued interpretation of succeeding librarians. We hope that the future will be as fruitful.

When the Exhibition appeared in 1976 I was able to thank a number of those who shared the work. Diana Steimle, Eva Stigers, Susan Danforth, and Richard Hurley contributed to making that first effort possible. John Alden brought felicitous hand and felicitous phrase to it. Thomas R. Adams, Librarian of the John Carter Brown Library, offered encouragement, freedom, and critical suggestions of the text which are greatly appreciated. I thank them all once again.

At that time I encouraged readers to "offer corrections, improvements, or appropriate observations so that in its next stage, the Catalogue will be more worthy of its subject." A number of readers responded: Giuseppe Billanovich, Jeannette Black, Elizabeth Cometti, Franco Fido, Anthony Molho, Anthony Oldcorn, Antonio Pace, Bernard Rosenthal, Robert Rosenthal and the students of his seminar at the University of Chicago, and John Tedeschi all made contributions. Classes of schoolchildren who visited the Exhibition asked questions which helped me to recognize places which needed expansion or clarifying. The Lilio (number 18) was added to the Exhibition for them. My wife, Penelope, helped prepare the index, she read and helped clarify an early draft of this text, and she has tolerated many evenings given in its fruition. Mrs. Raymond Watts, the Library's invaluable "Doppie," took the manuscript home and applied red pencil to the text's benefit and the reader's gain. Susan James Demers and Lynne Southwick bore the typing of this cheerfully. I thank them all and only regret that I cannot ask them to share the blame for the mistakes which you, reader, must inevitably find. I ask that you be forgiving and again ask you to offer your corrections, improvements, or appropriate observations.

When Vincent Buonanno and I planned this, we decided to seek financial support from our community to pay the necessarily high printing costs. The work involved in that effort has been considerable and the time consumed extensive. It has been gratifying to have received the support we have. At a time when it has become almost automatic to turn to agencies of the federal government for support of such publications, it is reassuring to know that there are individuals in the community who are concerned enough about our heritage to contribute to a publication of this kind. A grant from the government might have been a faster way of accomplishing our goals, but I would have missed meeting the fine people who participated in this and would have missed making many friends. I thank the Committee members who spent their valuable time and staked their reputations on our behalf. And, finally, I thank the patrons who made this possible. I hope that they find their confidence in the project was warranted.

Samuel J. Hough
Assistant Librarian

List of Plates

COLOR

Endpapers   Vincenzo Scotti. Tavole delle ... bandiere. Leghorn, 1796. Cat. no. 127.

I   Vesconte Maggiolo. World Map. Naples, 1511. Cat. no. 101.

II   Battista Agnese. World Map. Venice, 1544. Cat. no. 104.

BLACK-AND-WHITE

I   Ptolemy manuscript. Southern Africa, [1440?] Cat. no. 5.

II   Columbus. Letter (first voyage). Rome, 1493. Cat. no. 6.

III   *Libretto* (Columbus's second and third voyages). Venice, 1504. Cat. no. 9.

IV   Vespucci. Letter. Paris, 1503. Cat. no. 11.

V   Vespucci. Dutch Letter. Antwerp, 1508. Cat. no. 16.

VI   Pigafetta. Magellan's voyage. Paris, 1525. Cat. no. 26.

VII   Montalboddo. *Paesi novamente retrovati*. Vicenza, 1507. Cat. no. 29.

VIII   Ramusio. First printed map of New England. Venice, 1556. Cat. no. 32.

IX   Bressani. *Nuova Francia*. Macerata, 1653. Cat. no. 54.

X   Hennepin. *Descrizione di Luigiana*. Bologna, 1686. Cat. no. 60.

XI   Gastaldi. *Universale Descrittione*. Venice, 1562. Cat. no. 108.

XII   Franklin. *Buon Uomo Ricciardo*. Venice, 1797. Cat. no. 87.

XIII   Alfieri. *L'America Libera*. Kehl, 1787. Cat. no. 91.

XIV   Bartolommeo da li Sonetti. World Map. Venice, 1532. [Map of ca. 1520.] Cat. no. 98.

XV Bordone. World Map. Venice, 1532. Cat. no. 99.

XVI Vavassore. World Map. [Venice, 1525?] Cat. no. 102.

XVII Ramusio. *Carta Universale*. Venice, 1534. Cat. no. 103.

XVIII "Florentine Goldsmith's Map." [Florence? 1544?] Cat. no. 106.

XIX Florian. Northern Hemisphere. Venice, 1556. Cat. no. 114.

XX Florian. Southern Hemisphere. Venice, 1556. Cat. no. 114.

XXI Fine. Cordiform World Map. [Venice, 1566.] Cat. no. 119.

XXII Gastaldi. *Universale*. Venice, 1546. Cat. no. 107.

XXIII Gastaldi. *Totius Orbis Descriptio*. [Venice, 1562–1569.] Cat. no. 110.

XXIV Olaus. Norse voyages. Rome, 1572. Cat. no. 113.

XXV Tramezino. New World. Venice, 1554. Cat. no. 112.

XXVI Tramezino. Old World. Venice, 1554. Cat. no. 112.

XXVII Forlani. South America. [Venice, ca. 1564–1572.] Cat. no. 115.

XXVIII Dudley. Map of New England. Florence, 1661. Cat. no. 125.

XXIX Coronelli. Gore of New England. Venice, 1705. Cat. no. 126.

Abbreviations of Works Cited Most Frequently

In the bibliographical notes to the entries we have used the following conventional forms.

JCBAR   The *John Carter Brown Annual Reports* printed from 1901 to 1968 (the issues through 1966 were reprinted, with an index, in 1972), cited by year and page; thus, JCBAR 13:19 means our *Report* for 1913, page 19.

JCB(3)1:52   The Library has published chronologically arranged catalogues of its contents. Editions were published in 1865–1872, 1882–1885, 1919–1931. Most recently, in 1973, we published a volume of our holding for 1675–1700. Citations refer to the edition, the part, and the page. In the case given here, to the third edition, first part (issued in 1919), page 52.

JCB *Collection's Progress*   The printed catalogue of an exhibition on the historical development of the Library, published in 1968.

Amat di S. Filippo   Pietro Amat di S. Filippo, *Biografia dei viaggiatori italiani colla bibliografia delle loro opere*. Second edition. Rome, 1882.

Backer   Augustin de Backer, *Bibliothèque de la Compagnie de Jésus*. Brussels, 1890–1952. Eleven volumes. Cited by volume and column.

Borba de Moraes   Rubens Borba de Moraes, *Bibliographia Brasiliana*, a bibliography of books about early Brazil in two volumes. Amsterdam, 1958. Cited by volume and page.

Church   Elihu Dwight Church, *A Catalogue of books relating to the Discovery and Early History of North and South America*. New York, 1907. Five volumes.

Colonial Scene   John Carter Brown Library, *The Colonial Scene (1602–1800)*. Worcester, 1950. The catalogue of an exhibition "augmented by related titles from the Library of the American Antiquarian Society."

Eames (Columbus)   Wilberforce Eames's discussion of editions of the Columbus letter in *Two important gifts to the New York Public Library*. New York, 1924.

Europe Informed   International Colloquium on Luso-Brazilian Studies, Sixth, Cambridge, Mass., and New York, 1966. *Europe Informed; an exhibition of early books which acquainted Europe with the East*. Cambridge, Mass., 1966.

Evans   Charles Evans, *American bibliography*. Chicago, 1903–1959. Twelve volumes. This is a chronological history of books printed in what is now the United States 1639–1800. Numbered serially.

Fite and Freeman   Emerson Fite and Archibald Freeman, *A book of old maps, delineating American history from the earliest days*. Cambridge, Mass., 1926.

Ford (*Franklin*)   Paul Leicester Ford, *Franklin Bibliography*. Brooklyn, N.Y., 1889.

Gamba   Bartolommeo Gamba, *Serie dei testi di lingua e di altre opere importante nella italiana letteratura*. Fourth edition. Venice, 1839.

Garrison-Morton   Fielding Hudson Garrison, *Garrison and Morton's medical bibliography*. London, 1954.

Gerbi, *Dispute*   Antonello Gerbi, *The Dispute of the New World*. Translated by Jeremy Moyle. Pittsburgh, 1973.

Goff   Frederick R. Goff, *Incunabula in American Libraries; a third census*. New York, 1964.

Harrisse (BAV)   Henry Harrisse, *Bibliotheca americana vetustissima*. New York, 1866.

Medina, *Lima*   José Toribio Medina, *La Imprenta en Lima*. Santiago de Chile, 1904–1907. Four volumes.

Pace, *Franklin*   Antonio Pace, *Benjamin Franklin and Italy*. Philadelphia, 1958.

Penrose, *Travel and Discovery*   Boies Penrose, *Travel and Discovery in the Renaissance*, Cambridge, Mass., 1952.

Sabin   Joseph Sabin, *Bibliotheca Americana: a dictionary of Books relating to America*. New York, 1868–1936. Twenty-nine volumes. Numbered serially.

Streit   Robert Streit, *Bibliotheca Missionum*. Münster, 1916–1966. This is cited by volume and its number within the volume; thus, 16:4486 is number 4486 in volume 16.

Tooley   R. V. Tooley, "Maps in Italian Atlases of the Sixteenth Century," in *Imago Mundi*, III (1939), pp. 12–47.

Wagner (N.W.)   Henry R. Wagner, *The Cartography of the Northwest Coast of America*. Berkeley, 1937. Two volumes.

World Encompassed   Baltimore Museum of Art, *The World encompassed; an exhibition of the history of maps*. Baltimore, 1952.

Wroth, *Verrazzano*   Lawrence C. Wroth, *The Voyage of Giovanni da Verrazzano, 1524–1528*. New Haven, Yale University Press, 1970.

THE ITALIANS
AND THE CREATION
OF AMERICA

The standard form of our descriptions is as follows.

MAIN ENTRY We have used the form of names and corporate bodies as they appear in our card catalogue. Whenever possible an author's dates have been included as they provide more exact identification and a clue, sometimes, to his age when the text appeared.

TITLE We have followed the Library's practice of making a quasi-facsimile transcription. The first letter of a word is capitalized in transcription if that letter in the book is a capital. All other letters are transcribed as lowercase.

IMPRINT We have transcribed the imprints by the same standard used for titles. Information derived from the colophon statement is so indicated. Information derived from external sources or in a form other than its appearance in the book appears in brackets. We have abbreviated some imprints and added punctuation where clarity rather than strict consistency seemed appropriate.

CITATIONS We have provided bibliographical citations to our own publications, to other bibliographies, and to appropriate books and articles in order that those who wish to verify our statements or learn more about the books may be assisted in the pursuit.

ACQUISITION INFORMATION We trust that our readers will find the date of acquisition and the benefactor of the Library interesting, and have provided that information to satisfy those as curious about such things as we are.

I *The Discovery of Discovery*

THE prominent part played by Marco Polo, Christopher Columbus, and the other Italians involved with new geographical discoveries is not an historical coincidence. The great explorers flourished in a society and a culture which produced attitudes and skills which these talented men required.

In the twelfth and thirteenth centuries the Italian city-republics had developed economies that generated surplus capital. Such inventions as double-entry bookkeeping and letters of credit enabled Italian bankers to manage money and direct it to constructive and profitable use. Europeans eagerly sought Italian capital, and Italian merchants and bankers were attracted to all the commercial centers of the West. But investments made beyond their own jurisdictions were dangerous: not only were there normal commercial risks, but they lacked political protection beyond their own city. Intelligence and training were required for survival: Italian businessmen were trained to calculate instantly, judge shrewdly, observe broadly, and reason acutely. These skills—the genius of Italy—permeated all levels of cultures: they were as much a part of the manner in which Italians looked at paintings as they were of Italian methods of looking at new lands and new maps.

1 MARCO POLO, 1254–1323

... *In Cui Si Tratta Le Meravigliose cose del mondo per lui vedute, del costume di varii paesi....*

In Venetia ... per Mathio Pagan ... [1555].

The Venetian merchant Marco Polo went to China in 1271. The tale of his travels was rich in detail, shrewd in judgment, filled with stories of adventure, danger, and wealth. While Marco Polo shared the outlook and skills of his class, his experiences resembled those in tales of chivalry. Many Venetians found the wonders he described to be beyond belief: the distances he traveled were greater than the extent of the whole world known or imagined at the time; the peoples he described were not described by anyone else; the wealth he encountered surpassed imagination. His book was called *Il Milione* because there were so many superlatives in it. But the book was enormously popular; nearly 200 copies of the manuscript survive. When travel to China turned out to be but an interlude—early in the fourteenth century the rising power of the Tartars in Central Asia created a barrier through which no European could safely enter—Marco Polo's vivid stories kept alive the memory of China and stimulated later explorers to seek a route to Cathay.

JCB(3)1:189; Sabin 44498; Leonardo Olschki, *The Genius of Italy*, Oxford, 1949, p. 370; Marco Polo, *The Description of the World*, edited by A. C. Moule and Paul Pelliot, 2 volumes, London, 1938.
Acquired after 1865, before 1875, by John Carter Brown.

With the closing of the routes to China, Europe—bounded to the south and east by the aggressive, imperialistic forces of Islam—was placed on the defensive and confined to an area which was continually shrinking. To the west lay the inhospitable Atlantic. During the fifteenth century, by mastering the ways of sailing ships across the ocean, Europeans transformed the Atlantic from a barrier to a highway. In doing so they gained an initiative in the world arena which has lasted through this century.

Prince Henry the Navigator, of Portugal, seeking to outflank the hostile Moors of North Africa, sent ships to explore the Atlantic coast of Africa. Mastery of the skills required to sail ships across seas over great distances out of sight of land was achieved gradually. Attitudes had to be changed, old fears overcome, and ships developed to meet the challenge. The maritime technology of the Mediterranean was melded with that of the Baltic–North Atlantic to create a new kind of ship and a new kind of sailing.

2 ALVISE DA CÀ DA MOSTO, 1432–1488
De Aloysii Cadamusti Itineribus Ad Terras Incognitas.
Colophon: Impressum Venetiis apud March. Sessam Cura . . . M.D.XV [1515].

By 1450 Portuguese explorers had reached the Senegal River. When Prince Henry encountered financial difficulties in 1451 and 1452 he allowed Italian merchants to participate in the African trading monopoly. It was with ships of Italian traders that the young Venetian Cà da Mosto made two voyages to the Senegal/Gambia region in 1455 and 1456. Cà da Mosto's account of those voyages was the first description of sub-Saharan Africa by a European. The young Italian was curious about how other people lived and had an eye for detail. He wrote of the flora, of the customs of the people, and in a lively style conveyed a sense of the way of life there. Iberian noblemen, more concerned with honor and glory, did not perceive the quality of other cultures and wrote largely of their own exploits when placed in similar circumstances. This is the only recorded separately printed edition of Cà da Mosto's account. It had appeared as part of Fracanzano de Montalboddo's *Paesi novamente retrovati*, Vicenza, 1507 (see number 29), and in six subsequent editions of Montalboddo prior to 1515.

Le Navigazioni Atlantiche di Alvise Da Cà Da Mosto, Rinaldo Caddeo, ed., Milan, 1929; John H. Parry, *The Discovery of the Sea*, New York, 1974, pp. 113–115.
Acquired 1968. Associates of the John Carter Brown Library.

The Renaissance in Italy was characterized by a desire to recover the knowledge of the classical world which had been lost in subsequent centuries. The Italian humanists hoped at first that the classical geographers knew about remote areas of the world of which they were ignorant. As lost works became available they were invaluable in providing analytic procedures which advanced the quality of geographical inquiry. But the information of the ancients on remote parts of the world was inconsistent and undependable, and, as travelers' reports about India and Africa arrived in Italy during the fifteenth century, geographers questioned the classical writers. As the century progressed, geographers became more confident in relying upon recent information.

3 CLAUDIUS PTOLEMAEUS
Cosmographia.
Bologna [1477].

The works of the geographer Ptolemy (lived second century A.D.) became available to Italy in 1406 when a Florentine merchant, Palla Strozzi, paid to have a Greek manuscript translated into Latin. Ptolemy provided the concept of a grid system for geographical measurement as well as the mathematical procedures for measuring the size of the earth and for making maps of large land areas. Ptolemy also determined the latitudes of locations throughout the Mediterranean area. He tried as well to approximate exact locations of sites in more remote regions of the world. Italian scholars adopted Ptolemy's rigorous mathematical system as a basis for their own studies. Just as Florentine artists combined a mastery of abstract principles of mathematical perspective with a grasp of practical, empirical elements to create a new kind of painting, so too the humanistic scholars combined the technical, mathematical procedures of Ptolemy with the increasingly available records of travelers' observations to create a new analytical geography. This is the first edition of Ptolemy with maps and it is the first book to be illustrated with copperplate engravings. The world map shows Ptolemy's second-century concept of a land mass connecting Africa and Asia, making the Indian Ocean an enclosed sea, which was the starting point of fifteenth-century discussions of the remote islands.

JCB(3)1:11; JCB *Collection's Progress* 47; Sabin 66471; R. A. Skelton, "Bibliographical Note" to facsimile published Amsterdam, 1963, by Theatrum Orbis Terrarum; *World Encompassed*, 34 (plate x); Samuel Y. Edgerton, "Florentine interest in Ptolemaic cartography as background for renaissance painting, architecture, and the discovery of America," *Journal of the Society of Architectural Historians*, XXXIII, Dec. 1974, pp. 275–292.

Acquired 1900 by John Nicholas Brown, the donor.

4 AENAEUS SILVIUS PICCOLOMINI (POPE PIUS II), 1405–1464
Cosmographia Pii Papae in Asiae & Europae eleganti descriptione....
Colophon: Impressa est ... per Henricum Stephanum impressorem diligentiss. Parrhisiis ... M.D.IX [1509].

The fomenting of geographical thought begun with the translation of Ptolemy into Latin was further stimulated by the Council of Florence, convened in 1439 to resolve differences between the Eastern Church and Rome. The Patriarch of Constantinople and the Pope sent their most learned representatives to consider the theological and historical issues separating them. We know that among the discussions of the Church scholars there were extensive exchanges on geographical subjects. The Byzantines preferred Strabo, the Greek geographer, whose descriptive style has led his book to be called a "glorified gazetteer." The divergent viewpoints of East and West, Strabo and Ptolemy, enlivened and richened the discussions about geography. The discoveries also attracted new information. In 1441 a priest brought Niccolo Conti, a Venetian merchant, to the Council. Conti had recently returned from India and Indo-China where he had lived for twenty-five years. His story was listened to with keen interest and was recorded by Poggio Bracciolini, the Papal Secretary.

The Sienese Piccolomini (he was elected Pope in 1458) wrote the one book which attempted to synthesize Italian geographical thought on remote regions in the period after the Council of Florence. Piccolomini's book on Asia, which circulated in manuscript after 1461, was based on Ptolemy, but many things had to be modernized: the world was clearly bigger than Ptolemy had calculated it to be, and the reports of travelers such as Marco Polo and Niccolo Conti had to be considered. Among other new ideas, Piccolomini concluded that Ptolemy's idea of a closed Indian Ocean was wrong. His book on Asia was first printed in a larger work, *Historia rerum ubique gestarum*, Venice, 1477. This is the first separately-printed edition of his geographical writings, edited by Geoffrey, Tory who recognized that Piccolomini had perceived important geographical concepts a half-century before they could be verified by voyages.

A. A. Renouard, *Annales de l'imprimerie des Estienne* . . . , Paris, 1843, p. 6, no. 3; Penrose, *Travel and Discovery*, p. 10.
Acquired 1969. Benefactors of the John Carter Brown Library.

5 CLAUDIUS PTOLEMAEUS
   [Atlas of 15 Maps. Italy, ca. 1440.]
   Manuscript on vellum and in color.

This collection of Ptolemaic maps contains one map of southern Africa that is decidedly un-Ptolemaic. First, southern Africa is not an area portrayed in any other recorded Ptolemaic map collection. Second, it does not present the Ptolemaic notion of a closed Indian Ocean, as do all the world maps in every other recorded manuscript and the editions of Ptolemy printed before 1490. Instead, it is one of the handful of maps, made before Vasco da Gama sailed around the Cape of Good Hope to India, which show Africa surrounded by ocean. In fact, it could be the earliest such map. It may have been made about the time of the Council of Florence and may reflect ideas generated there. It certainly reflects the ambiance of Quattrocento Italy when the ideas of the classical world were recovered, examined, and questioned, and when accepted concepts were revised or rejected.

Plate I.

JCBAR 52:43–52; JCB *Collection's Progress* 101, plate XXXIV; Joseph Fischer, *Codex Urbinas Graecus 82, Tomus Prodomus*, 526–527, no. L40*; Leo Bagrow, "The Wilczek-Brown Codex," *Imago Mundi*, XII, 1955, pp. 171–174; Wilcomb E. Washburn, "Representation of unknown lands in XIV-, XV-, and XVI-century cartography," *Agrupamento de Estudos de Cartografia Antiga*, Coimbra, 1969, p. 7.
Acquired 1952. Associates of the John Carter Brown Library.

II *Columbus*

THE geographical questions that Columbus asked represent the culmination of an intellectual process that had begun and flourished in Italy. Columbus had read the books of Marco Polo and Pius II (from whom he learned his Ptolemy) as well as those of other geographers. He had obtained a copy of a letter written in 1474 by Paolo del Pozzo Toscanelli, the leading Florentine geographer, who thought a western ocean passage to China was feasible. He knew merchants and pilots who had sailed the African coast. From his reading and discussion Columbus became convinced that Asia could be reached by sailing to the West. Ships and navigation had advanced to such a point that long oceanic voyages became possible. In the summer of 1492 Spain's political situation enabled the release of funds to pay for the ships Columbus needed. He had the opportunity of proving his theory. When he encountered land where he had projected Japan to be, Columbus believed that he had demonstrated his idea to be correct.

6 CRISTOFORO COLOMBO, 1446/51–1506
Epistola Christofori Colom: cui etas nostra multum debet: de Insulis Indie supra Gangem nuper inventis. . . .
[Rome, Stephen Plannck, May 1493.]

As he returned to Spain in February of 1493, Columbus composed an account which was to serve as the public announcement of his discovery. It was not addressed to any particular individual but was enclosed with a letter, now lost, to the Spanish sovereigns. They had manuscript transcriptions made of Columbus's account and distributed these to court officials. One of these transcripts, endorsed to Luis de Santangel, was printed in Spanish at Barcelona in April 1493. From a better and more accurate manuscript, Leandro de Cosco made a Latin translation, giving it the title *Epistola* or "letter," by which it has been known ever since. The translation was sent to Rome and in May the first Latin edition was published. It is this Italian publication which informed Europe of Columbus's discoveries.

Plate II.

JCB(3)1:19; JCB *Collection's Progress* 19; Eames (Columbus) 3; Goff c757; Samuel E. Morison, *Admiral of the Ocean Sea*, Boston, 1942 (see volume 1, pp. 413–414; vol. 2, pp. 32–45).
Acquired 1846 by John Carter Brown.

7 [CRISTOFORO COLOMBO], 1446/51–1506
De Insulis inventis Epistola Cristoferi Colom. . . .
[Basel, Michael Furter, for Johann Bergmann, 1493.]

Columbus's letter appeared in nine Latin editions. After the first, there were two more editions printed at Rome in 1493. Printers in other countries copied the Rome editions; three were printed at Paris and one at Antwerp. The present Basel edition is the first to be illustrated. The local artist who executed the woodcuts portrayed Columbus's ships as oared galleys. There was one other edition printed in Basel in 1494 as part of another book.

The John Carter Brown Library possesses six of the nine Latin editions of the Columbus letter. By doing so we can demonstrate the way in which the news of Columbus's discovery was presented and also the extent to which the news spread across Europe.

JCB(3)1:18; JCB *Collection's Progress* 41; Eames (Columbus) 7; Goff c760.
Acquired 1896 by John Nicholas Brown, the donor.

8 CRISTOFORO COLOMBO, 1446/51–1506
Eyn schön hübsch lesen von etlichen insslen die do in Kurtzen zyten funden synd durch dē Künig von hispania. ...
   Colophon: Getruckt zü straszburg uff gruneck võ meister Bartolomesz Küstler [i.e., Kistler] ym iar: M.CCCC. xcvii. [1497].

The Latin Columbus letter was translated into German and printed in one edition of 1497. It was also translated into Tuscan verse by the Florentine poet Giuliano Dati. Five editions of the poem have been identified, the first printed at Rome in June 1493, the other four at Florence in October of the same year. They are very rare: four are known in single copies (one of which is incomplete) and the fifth is known in two copies.

JCB(3)1:29; Eames (Columbus) 12; Sabin 14638; Goff c762.
Acquired 1851 by John Carter Brown.

9 [PIETRO MARTIRE D'ANGHIERA], 1457–1526
Libretto De Tutta La Navigatione De Re De Spagna De Le Isole Et Terreni Novamente Trovati.
   Colophon: Stampado in Venesia per Albertino Vercellese da Lisona a di X de aprile. M. CCCCC. iiii [1504].

Columbus's second voyage (October 1493 – June 1496) and third voyage (May 1498 – October 1500) to America were largely concerned with the colonization of Hispaniola. The period began with high hopes and ended with Columbus being sent home in chains. This little book was the first published account of those voyages. Pietro Martire d'Anghiera (on whom see number 30) included an original narrative of the third voyage and the earliest physical description of Columbus himself. This is one of the most important books on the discovery period, as well as one of the rarest: only two other copies are known.

Plate III.

JCB(3)1:39; JCB *Collection's Progress* 67; L. C. Wroth, "Introduction" to *Libretto de Tutta la Navigatione de Re de Spagna* ... *A Facsimile* ... , Paris, 1929.
Acquired 1904. Endowment funds.

10 CRISTOFORO COLOMBO, 1446/51–1506
[*Manuscript extracts of his capitulations with King Ferdinand and Queen Isabella.*]
[Spain, November 1504 or after.]

This manuscript is a contemporary summary of the privileges Columbus received from Ferdinand and Isabella between the years 1492 and 1502. As discoverer of the West Indies, Columbus sought and was granted grandiose titles, such as Admiral of the Ocean Sea, which reflected his ambition to obtain feudal control in lands he discovered. As the dimensions of his discoveries became apparent and the crown became aware of the consequent power that he would command, the monarchs—whose life work was consolidating power and reducing feudal privilege—refused to allow Columbus the absolute authority and revenues in the New World he thought were his. This document asserts Columbus's claims as they existed after the fourth voyage. It was compiled either by him at the end of his life or by his heirs shortly after his death. Generations of his descendants tried, with very limited success, to obtain his privileges. A century and a half later they were given Jamaica as a settlement. In 1655 an English invasion took even that from them.

JCB(3)1:16; S. De Ricci, *Census of Medieval and Renaissance Manuscripts in the United States and Canada* (1937), vol. II, pp. 2145–46.
Acquired 1890 by John Nicholas Brown, the donor.

III *Vespucci*

AMERIGO VESPUCCI may not have been the first to realize that a new continent had been discovered, but his letters were the first revelations of that startling fact that were read by a large audience throughout Europe. The letters attracted readers not only because of the news of a New World, but because of their vivid descriptions of the cannibalism and sexual promiscuity of the natives. Vespucci placed himself at the center of action and attention and this brought him rapid and lasting fame, but it also makes him, in Samuel Eliot Morison's words, "the most controversial character in the history of discovery."

Vespucci was born in Florence in 1451 of a leading family and worked for the Medici bank from his youth. In 1491 the bank sent him to work in its Seville affiliate where he was a merchant banker and ship chandler. As chandler, at the port from which Columbus and all the following Spanish voyagers to America set sail and to which they returned, Vespucci had detailed information about the earliest voyages of discovery. Vespucci made three voyages to America. In 1499 he accompanied a Spaniard, Alonso de Hojeda, who sailed along the Spanish Main. Then, forbidden to sail in a Spanish ship, he went out as a member of two Portuguese fleets both commanded by Gonçalo Coelho in 1501–1502 and again in 1503. What makes Vespucci so controversial is that he claimed to have made an earlier voyage, in 1497—a voyage which only his keenest partisans have believed ever took place. Furthermore, he wrote as if he had led the three voyages he did go on—he gave credit to no one but himself, and this discredited him among his contemporaries beginning with Sebastian Cabot in 1515.

11 AMERIGO VESPUCCI, 1451–1512
Albericus vespuccius laurentio petri francesci de medicis Salutem, pluriman dicit.
[Paris, Felix Baligault and Jehan Lambert, 1503.]

After returning from his Portuguese voyage, 1501–1502, Amerigo Vespucci sent a letter from Lisbon to his former employer, Lorenzo di Pier Francesco de' Medici of Florence. The Portuguese ships had sailed down the coast of Brazil for hundreds of miles before turning east and returning home. The mass of land as well as the prodigious flow of the Amazon clearly indicated that they were passing no mere islands off the coast of Asia. In his letter Vespucci was emphatic about that. What Lorenzo de' Medici did with the original manuscript we do not know, as the original is lost. He did send a copy to Paris. There, Fra Giovanni Giocondo of Verona, residing in Paris as royal architect to King Louis XII, made a Latin translation of it. It was Giocondo's translation that was first printed.

Plate IV.

JCB(3)1:40; Sabin 99327; Harrisse (BAV) 26.
Acquired 1854 by John Carter Brown.

12   AMERIGO VESPUCCI, 1451–1512

Mundus Novus.

[Venice, Giovanni Baptista Sessa, 1504.]

The second edition of Vespucci's letter was printed in Venice. The printer, Sessa, used Fra Giovanni Giocondo's Latin version of the text, as printed the preceding year in Paris. Sessa emended the text and gave it the title *Mundus Novus*, "New World." With this title the work spread quickly throughout Europe. The discovery of a new world was of greater news value than the discovery of a new route to the known East, and contributed to the fact that Vespucci's letter had wider circulation in the years 1503–1508 than Columbus's letter had enjoyed a decade earlier.

JCB(3)1:39; Sabin 99328.
Acquired 1850 by John Carter Brown.

13   AMERIGO VESPUCCI, 1451–1512

Mundus Novus.

Colophon: Magister johañes otmar: vin delice impressit Auguste Anno Millesimo quingentesimo quarto [1504].

The third edition of the Vespucci letter was printed in Augsburg. Augsburg was the first major commercial city on the German side of the Alps on the trade route through the Brenner Pass from Venice. Venetian goods had been carried in barrels by mule packs across that route for centuries before printing was introduced. When Venice grew to become the leading center of printing in Europe in the 1470's, barrels filled with sheets of book pages were added to the loads heading north. In this case Johann Otmar, a printer in Augsburg, reprinted the edition that had appeared in Venice. In the centuries that followed much of the news of America passed to Germany by this route.

JCB(3)1:39; Sabin 99330; Harrisse (BAV) 31.
Acquired 1846 by John Carter Brown.

14   AMERIGO VESPUCCI, 1451–1512
Mundus Novus
[Rome, Eucharius Silber, 1504.]

The Roman printer who published one of the three Roman editions of the Columbus letter, Eucharius Silber, made further textual alterations in the Vespucci text as modified at Venice, and added a title page. This form of the text was the basis of later Latin editions printed at Nuremberg, Strassburg, Rostock, Cologne, and Antwerp. Even later Paris editions follow this "Roman" text rather than the text of the original Parisian edition.

JCB(3)1:40; Sabin 99331.
Acquired 1854 by John Carter Brown.

15   AMERIGO VESPUCCI, 1451–1512
Von der neü gefunden Region so wol ein welt genempt mag werden....
[Basel, Michael Furter, 1505.]

European demand for news of Vespucci's discoveries is reflected here. This is one of two German translations published in twelve different editions at Basel, Munich, Nuremberg, Strassburg, Leipzig, and Magdeburg. These twelve editions contrast with the single German printing of the Columbus letter and reveal how much more extensive was Vespucci's reputation at the time.

JCB(3)1:41; Sabin 99340; Harrisse (BAV) 37.
Acquired before 1865 by John Carter Brown.

16   AMERIGO VESPUCCI, 1451–1512
Van de nieuwer werelt....
Colophon: Gheprent Thantwerpen ... Bi Jan van Doesborch [1508].

The Vespucci letter was also translated into Dutch and printed at Antwerp. The John Carter Brown copy is the only one recorded. The Dutch edition is noteworthy for Hans Burgkmair's illustrations of natives. Burgkmair's blocks were carried to Venice and were used a century later to illustrate an edition of Giovanni Botero, *Le Relationi universali*, printed there in 1618 and again in 1622.

Plate V.

JCB(3)1:48; JCB *Collection's Progress* 22, plate IV; Sabin 99352; Walter Fraser Oakeshott, *Some Woodcuts by Hans Burgkmair*, Oxford, Printed for presentation to the members of the Roxburghe Club, 1960.
Acquired 1871 by John Carter Brown.

In 1505 a letter by Vespucci was published at Florence. This one was addressed to Piero Soderini, Gonfaloniere of the Florentine Republic, who had been Vespucci's schoolmate. In it Vespucci describes four voyages he made to America—including the fictitious one of 1497. Circulation of this letter was peculiar. No other Italian edition is recorded, but parts of it appeared in German as broadsides—and it was translated into Czech. The most influential publication of the Soderini letter was in Latin in the book described in the following entry.

17   MARTIN WALDSEEMÜLLER, 1470–1521?
Cosmographiae Introductio...
Colophon: Urbs Deodate [Saint-Dié, France, 1507].

The word "America" first appeared in this work by Waldseemüller, a German geographer then teaching at Saint-Dié in the mountainous Vosges region of eastern France. Waldseemüller admired Vespucci's accomplishments and published a Latin translation of his letter to Piero Soderini. Waldseemüller did not realize that the new land Vespucci described was the same as the Asian Islands found by Columbus. The geographer proposed to name the "mundus novus" for its presumed discoverer. We should call it America, from the Latin form of Vespucci's first name, Americus, he wrote, for as Europe and Asia were named for women, America could be named for a man. The name spread quickly and was soon in wide use, and when Waldseemüller became aware of his error and tried to correct his mistake, it was already too late.

> Nūc vo & hę partes sunt latius lustratæ/& alia quarta pars per Americū Vesputiū(vt in sequentibus audietur)inuenta est/quā non video cur quis iure vetet ab Americo inuentore sagacis ingenij vi
> **America** ro Amerigen quasi Americi terrā / siue Americam dicendā: cū & Europa & Asia a mulieribus sua sortita sint nomina. Eius situ & gentis mores ex bis binis Americi nauigationibus quæ sequunt liquide intelligi datur.

JCB(3)1:45; Harrisse (BAV) 45; Harold Jantz, "Images of America in the German Renaissance," *First Images of America: The Impact of the New World on the Old*, Los Angeles, 1976, vol. 1, pp. 91–106 (esp. pp. 96–100).
Acquired 1846 by John Carter Brown.

IV   *The Impact of the Discoveries upon Italy*

THE discovery of a new world broke down centuries-old concepts which Europeans held concerning the earth they lived on. As ideas about the relationship of the parts of the earth changed, so did ideas of the place of an individual on the earth and in the cosmos. This required adjustments not merely in geographical thinking but in metaphysical, political, and religious attitudes as well. This section includes books which reveal the way in which Italian thinkers confronted the breakdown of old ideas and worked to replace them with new.

18 ZACHARIAS LILIO, BISHOP, D. CA. 1522

... De origine & laudibus scientiarum ... Contra Antipodes ... De miseria hominis et contemptu mundi. ...

Colophon: Florence, Francesco Bonaccorsi for Pierro Pacini, April 1496.

In the seventh century A.D., Isidore, Bishop of Seville, drew a world map which shaped European geographical concepts for nine hundred years. It is simply a "T" inside an "O" (reproduced below). The upper half of the circle represented Asia, the lower two quarters Europe and Africa. The crossing of the "T," the center of the earth, was Jerusalem, the spiritual and historical center of Christian culture. The expansion of geographical knowledge broke down this world concept. How difficult the new concepts were to accept is shown in this Florentine book, published slightly more than three years after Columbus had returned. The Isidorian world map is still present in abstract form, and Bishop Lilio is skeptical about news of discoveries: "... unless anyone believes very extraordinary news that the King of Spain, so they say, is sending ships these days to explore new shores."

FIGVRA DVODECIM VENTORVM

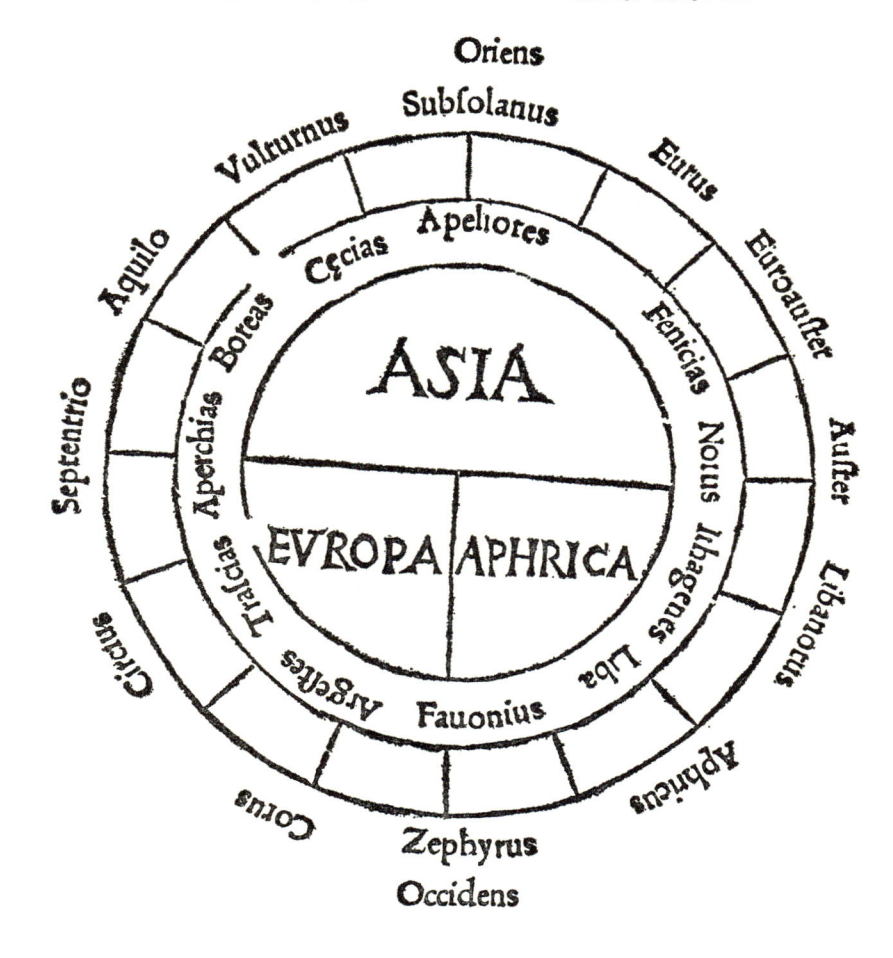

JCB(3)1:25; Harrisse (BAV) 17; Sabin 41067; *World Encompassed* 17.
Acquired 1903. Endowment funds.

[33]

19 CLAUDIUS PTOLEMAEUS

Geographia.

Rome, Bernardinus Venetus di Vitalibus, 1507.

In the sixteenth century, editors of Ptolemy attempted to reconcile Ptolemy's work with the discoveries of lands unknown to the classical geographer. The 1507 and 1508 editions of Ptolemy produced in Rome are noteworthy for the addition of a copperplate engraved map made by a German, Johannes Ruysch. The map is a planisphere on a conical projection with its apex at the North Pole. It contains an accurate Africa, an India whose mass is fully realized, and evidence of knowledge of the discoveries of both Columbus and Vespucci. This map, probably derived from a now-lost Italian manuscript, suggests what an heroic effort was involved when cartographers in the first years of the discoveries tried to make sense of the fragmented information that filtered back to Europe. The efforts of sixteenth-century Italian mapmakers to bring order to their maps is treated as a separate section at the end of this catalogue, but here we wish to show one of the important early maps and the difficulties its maker faced. On this map, Newfoundland appears as an Asian peninsula, South America as a disconnected island, and Hispaniola as an island near Japan. Ruysch, and his model, obviously had difficulties in understanding how reports of discoveries related one to the other.

JCB(3)1:44; JCBAR 59:33–37; Sabin 66475; Bradford F. Swan, "The Ruysch map of the world (1507–1508)," from *Papers of the Bibliographical Society of America*, vol. 45, n. 3, pp. 219-236; *World Encompassed* 53. Acquired 1959. The gift of George H. Beans.

One of the forces which most threatened and stimulated the European order was the power of Islam to the east and south. Italian traders were the Europeans most regularly in contact with the Islamic world, and Italy was the country most exposed to the naval power of Islamic rulers. The fact that the discovery and development of America were about to alter Europe in as extensive and radical a way as had the Crusades against Islam a few centuries before was not self-evident in 1500.

20 PIETRO PASQUALIGO, 1472–1515

. . . Ad Hemanvelem Lusitaniae Regem Oratio.

Colophon: Impressum Venetiis per Bernardinum Venetum de Vitalibus . . . M.CCCC.I. [1501].

For Italians the discovery of new lands and new routes to the Far East did not reduce the immediate threat that Turkish power presented in the Near East. In this oration the Venetian ambassador to Lisbon praises King Manuel profusely for the Portuguese discovery of new lands and peoples unknown to the ancients. But he admonishes Manuel not to allow the discoveries to distract Portugal from attending to the main threat of Europe: the power of the Turks in the eastern Mediterranean.

An English translation has been published by Donald Weinstein: *Ambassador from Venice: Pietro Pasqualigo in Lisbon, 1501*. Minneapolis, University of Minnesota Press [1960].
Acquired 1975. Endowment funds.

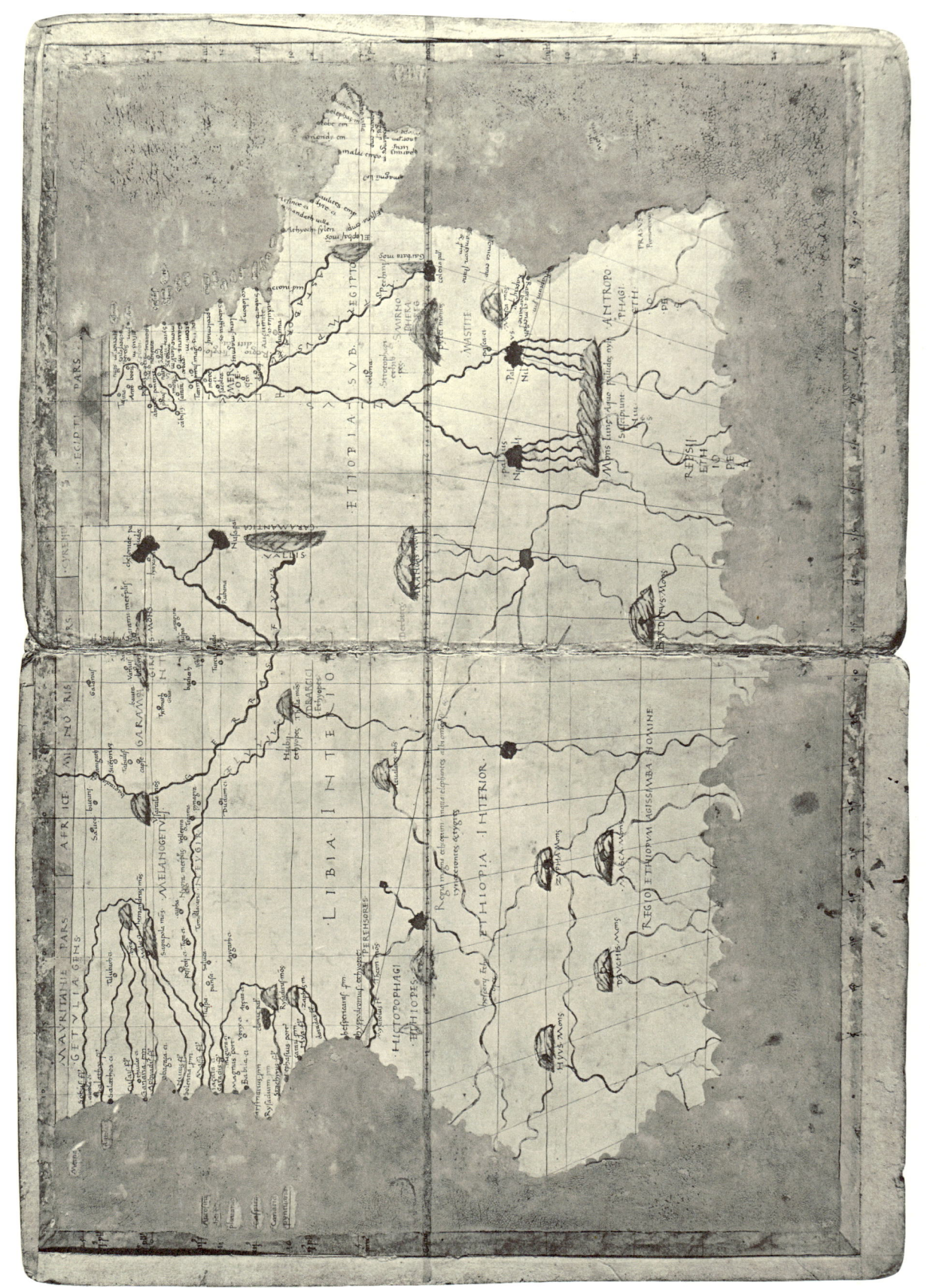

I (cat. no. 5) Ptolemy manuscript. Southern Africa, [1440?]. 56×39 cm.

II (cat. no. 6)   Columbus. Letter (first voyage). Rome, 1493. 17 × 11 cm. *Courtesy of Mr. and Mrs. Joseph Muratore.*

Libretto De Tutta La Nauigatione De Re De Spagna De Le Isole Et Terreni Nouamente Trouati. Capitulo primo:

CRISTOPHORO Colōbo Zenouese homo de alta & procera statura rosso de grande ingegno & faza longa. Sequito molto tempo li serenissimi Re de spagna in q̄ lunq̄ parte andauano: pcurādo lo aiutassero adarmare qualche nauilio: che se offeriua attouare p ponēte insule finitime de la india: doue e copia de pietre pciose: & & specie: & oro: che facilmēte se porriano cōsegre. Per molto tempo el Re & la Regina: & tutti li primati de Spagna: de zo ne pigliauano zocho: & finaliter dapo sette anni: & dapo molti trauagli. Cōpiacetteno a sua uolūta: & li armarno una naue & do carauelle cō leq̄le circa ali pmi zorni de septē.1492. se pti da li liti spani: & icomizo el suo uiazo. Ca.ii.

Rio da Cades se nādo alisole fortūate ch alpñte spagnoli lechi p amāo canarie: forno chiamate dali antiq isole fortūate nelmar oceā lōtan dal streto.1200.mi.secōdo sua rason che dicono.30. leghe: una lega e.4.migla. q̄ste canarie forō dcē fortūate p la loro tēpie. sono fora dl clia dela europa uerso mezo di. sono et habbitate de gēte nude ch uiuono senza religiōe alcūa, q̄ando colobo psar aq̄ & tor refrescamēto: pria chel se metesse a cosi dura fatiga, Deli sequēte elsole occidēte. Nauigādo.33. note & zorni cōtinui: ch mai uede terra alcūa. Dapoi un hō mōtato i gabia ueteno terra, Et descoprirno.vi.isole, Do de leq̄le de grādeza inaudita: una chiama spagnola: laltra la zoāna mela. Ca.iii.

Oāna nō hebero bē certo ch lafusse isola. Ma zōti ch foro ala zoāna scorēdo q̄lla p costa. Sētirono cātar del mese de nouēb. fra dēsissimi boschi rusignoli: & trouoro grandissimi fiumi de aque dolce: & bōissimi porti: & grādi scorēdo p costa de lazoāna p maistro piu de.800.migla che nō trouorn termie ne segno de termie: pēsoro ch fusse terra ferma: delibō de tornar: pch cosi elcōstrēgea ilmar: pch era ādato tāto p diuersi golfi: che hauea uolto la pua a septētriōe. Ita ch labora ormai licomizaua adar traualio: uolta aduq̄ la pua uerso leuāte: ritrouo lisola chiamata spagnola. Et dsiderādo tētar lanatura de li lochi da lapte d tramōtana: za se aproxiaua aterra: qn lanaue mazor inuesti sopra una secha piana: che era copta daq̄: & se aprite: ma laplanitie del sasso che staua sotto laq̄ laiuto che nō somerse: le carauelle scapolo li hoi: & esmōtati i terra uideo hoi d lisola liq̄li uisti subito se miseno a fugire aboschi dēsissimi: cōe fusseno tāte fiei seq̄tate dacāi (iaudita pgēia) li nri seq̄tādoli pso una dōna: & lamenorō anaue: e bē pasiuta d nri cibi & uso & ornata d uestimti ch loro tuti uāo nudi: la lassarno andar. Ca.iiii.

Subito ch so zōta asoi ch sauea oue stauāo: mōstrādo ilmarauigloso

A ii

III (cat. no. 9) *Libretto* (Columbus's second and third voyages). Venice, 1504. 19×12 cm. *Courtesy of the Columbus National Bank*

V (cat. no. 16) Vespucci. Dutch letter. Antwerp, 1508. 15×11 cm. *Courtesy of Mr. and Mrs. Ugo Gasbarro.*

IV (cat. no. 11) Vespucci. Letter. Paris, 1503. 19×11 cm.

VI (cat. no. 26) Pigafetta. Magellan's voyage. Paris, 1525. 15×10 cm.

VII (cat. no. 29) Montalboddo. *Paesi novamente retrovati.* Vicenza, 1507. 20×13 cm. *Courtesy of Mr. and Mrs. Robert Andreoli.*

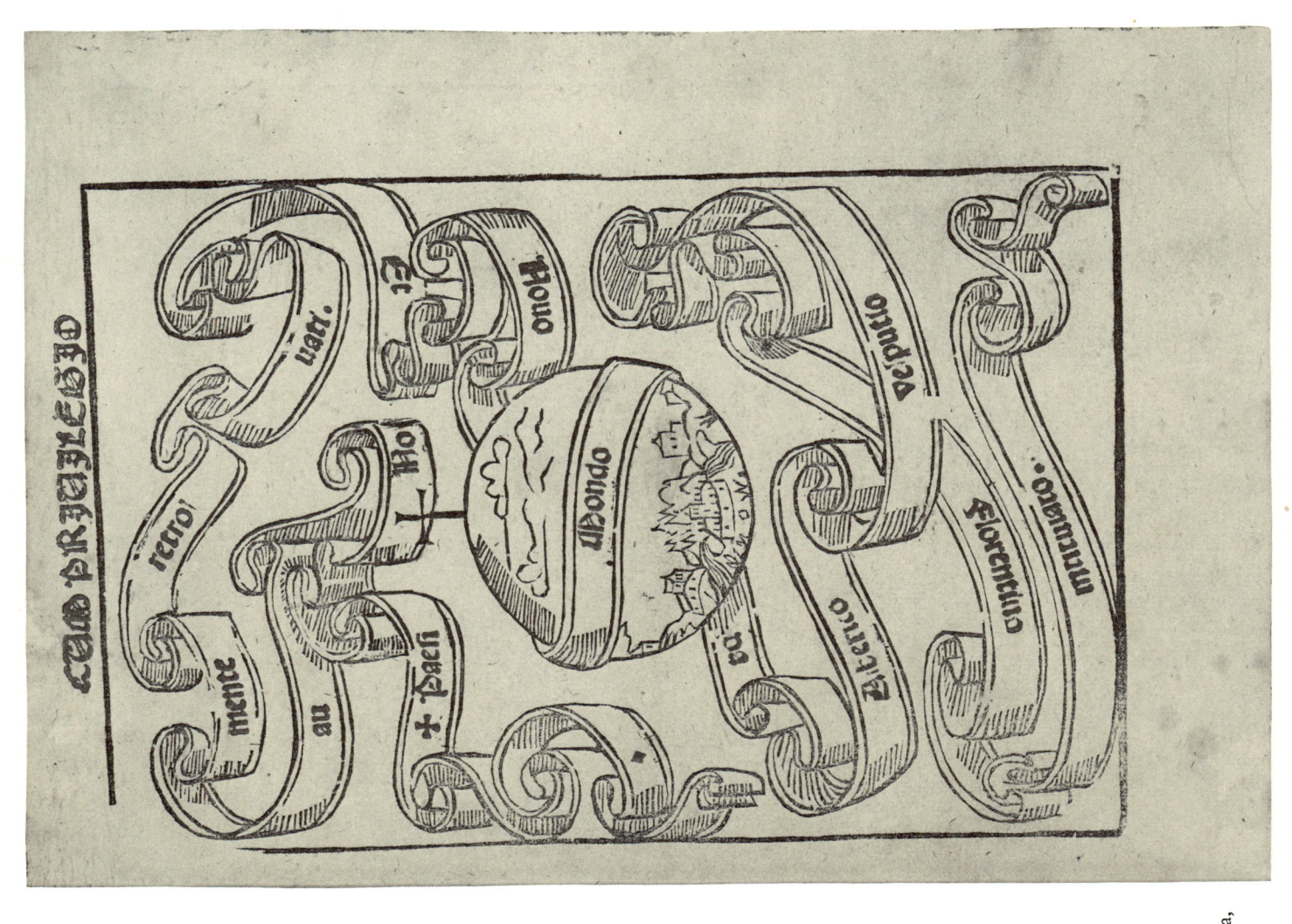

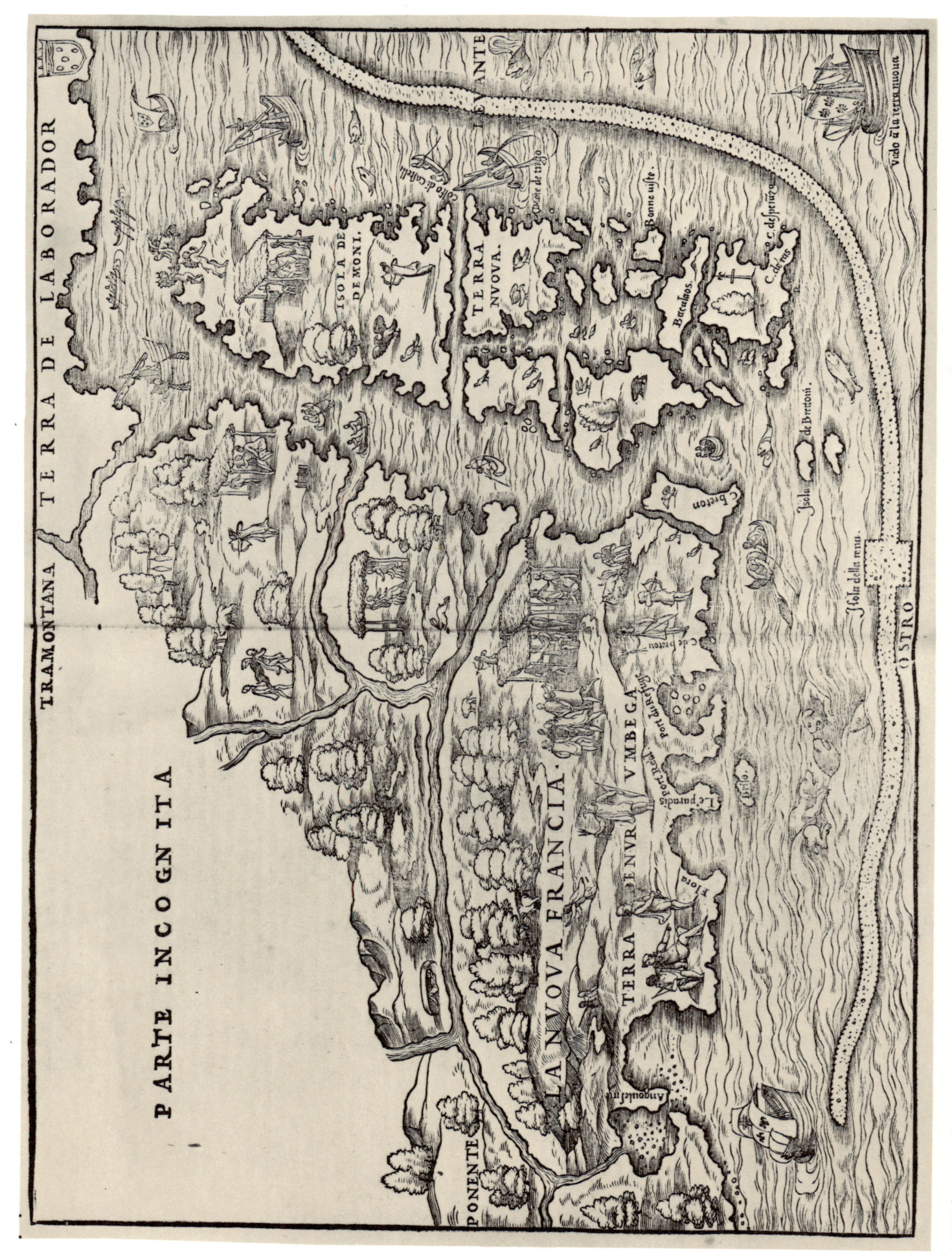

VIII (cat. no. 32) Ramusio. First printed map of New England. Venice, 1556. 29×38 cm. *Courtesy of the Grand Lodge of Rhode Island, Order of the Sons of Italy in America.*

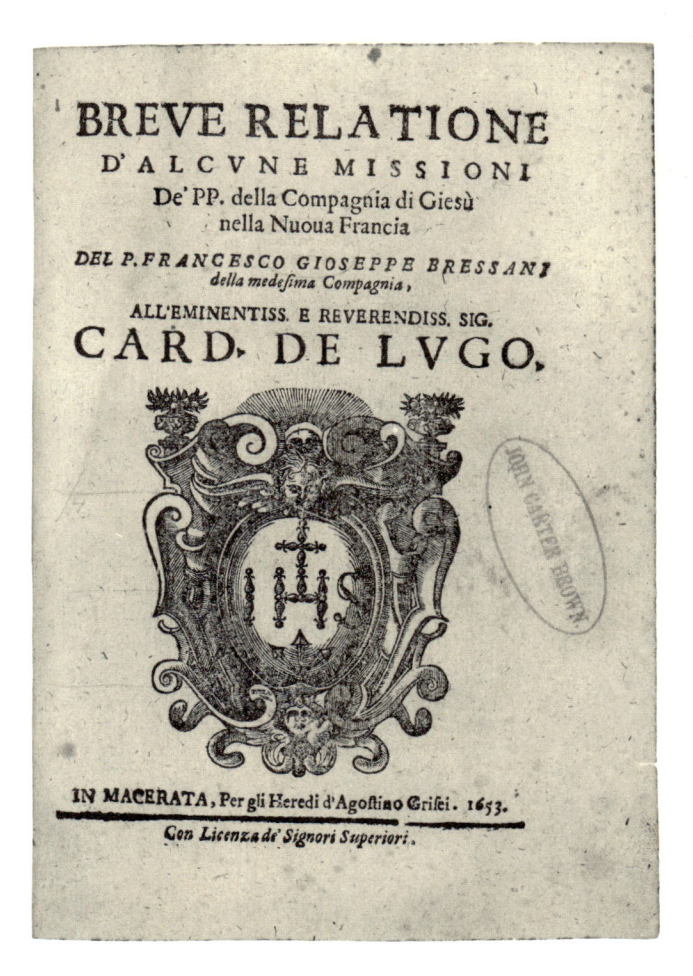

IX (cat. no. 54) Bressani. *Nuova Francia*. Macerata, 1653. 20×13 cm.

XI (cat no. 108) Gastaldi. *Universale Descrittione*. Venice, 1562. 14×10 cm.

X (cat. no. 60) Hennepin. *Descrizione di Luigiana*. Bologna, 1686. 13×7 cm. *Courtesy of Mr. and Mrs. Tempel Smith.*

XII (cat. no. 87) Franklin. *Buon Uomo Ricciardo*. Venice, 1797. 17×10 cm.

XIII (cat. no. 91) Alfieri. *L'America Libera*. Kehl, 1787. 21×14 cm. *Courtesy of Dr. and Mrs. Eugene Russo.*

21 GIOVANNI FRANCESCO PICO DELLA MIRANDOLA, 1470–1533

... *De Rerum Praenotione Libri Novem. Pro Veritate Religionis | Contra Superstitiosa Vanitates Editi.*

[Strassburg, Johann Knoblock, 1507.]

Count Pico was a philosopher as well as a ruler of the tiny dukedom of Mirandola near Modena. He believed that Columbus's "discovery" that the islands of "Asia" could be reached by sailing west might provide a potential base from which the Turks could be attacked from behind.

Adolf Schill, *Gianfrancesco Pico della Mirandola und die entdeckung Amerikas*, Berlin, 1929.
Acquired 1976. Endowment funds.

The discovery of people unaccounted for in the Bible or the writings of ancient authors was as much of a challenge to the limited world of Europe as were new lands and new oceans. Some of the ways Italians reacted to America and the role Italians played in shaping later attitudes are suggested below.

22 ISIDORO ISOLANO, D. 1528

... *In hoc volumine hec continentur De Imperio Militantis Ecclesiae libri quattuor.* ...

Colophon: Impressum Mediolani apud Gotardum Ponticum. Anno ... M.D.X.VII [1517].

As the extent of the western islands and their heathen populations became apparent to Europeans, a few in the Church realized that a great opportunity to extend its influence was presented them, that indeed they had an obligation to send missions. This book contains one of the first discussions of the implications of conversion after military conquest. The author, a Dominican theologian and native of Milan, was one of the men in the forefront of a realization of the consequences of the conquests in the New World.

Sabin 35264; Harrisse (BAV) additions 49; Streit 1:13.
Acquired 1976. Endowment funds.

23 JULIAN GARCÉS, BISHOP OF TLAXCALA, 1442?–1542

De Habilitate Et Capacitate Gentium Sive Indorum novi mundi.
Romae, Anno M.D.XXXVII [1537].

When Cortés conquered Mexico, Catholic Spain gained political control over more than 25 million natives. The "spiritual conquest" of these people which began in 1523 was of no less significance and was much more complicated. As the Spanish crown regarded the conversion of the Indians as justification for their rule, success was vital. But the Church had never satisfactorily resolved whether or not pagans could be saved. A strong tendency, derived from Aristotle, considered pagans "natural slaves" with no rights whatsoever. In Rome the leadership of the Church was faced with a moral decision: were the Indians capable of becoming Christians, and, if so, should their rights be protected before conversion was actually achieved?

This book, of which no other copy is recorded, is a letter from the Dominican Bishop of Tlaxcala in Mexico arguing strongly that the Indians were rational and spiritual beings capable of becoming Christians. Garcés urges the Pope to offer the protection of the Church to the lives and property of the native population. The letter was published as part of a campaign to convince Pope Paul III that he should act. Pope Paul responded by issuing his bull *Sublimus Deus* on 2 June 1537. This bull is a great and important document. It accepted Garcés's arguments and declared Indians "truly men." In forceful language Paul stated the Church's mission and offered the protection of Christ to all people.

Facsimile published by Lewis Hanke, "The theological significance of the discovery of America," *First Images of America*, Berkeley and Los Angeles, 1976, vol. 1, pp. 375–389; Harrisse (BAV) additions 12. Acquired 1969. Benefactors of the John Carter Brown Library.

> Ma quãto fuſſero felici i popoli ſenza queſti Sauii, ſi puo facilmente giudicar la vita, e i coſtumi de i popoli nouamente ritrouati nelle indie occidentali, i quali beati ſenza legge, ſenza lettere, e ſenza ſauii, non apprezauano ne oro, ne gioie non conoſceuano ne auaritia, ne ambitione, ne arte veruna, ſi nutriuano de i frutti che la terra ſenza arte produceua, haueuano ſi come nella Republica di Platone, ogni coſa comune, inſino alle donne, è i fanciulli chenaſceuano, come proprii comunemente nutriuam, & alleuauano, e quelli riconoſcẽdo tutti come padri, ſenza odio, ne paſſion alcuna, viueuano in perpetuo amor, e carita, ſi come nel ſecolo fortunato, e veramẽte d'oro dal vecchio Saturno, ilqual giocondo, e ripoſato viuere del tutto gli hanno ſturbato, et interrotto gli ambitioſi, e auari Spagnoli, liquali capitando in quelle ragiõi, col lor troppo ſapere, e con leggi duriſſime, non altramente che ſe'l boſſolo di Pandora portato v'haueſſero, di mille ſquadre di noie, e di mali gli hanno riempiti.

24. Passage from Albergati's *La Pazzia*.

24 [VIANESIO ALBERGATI]
La Pazzia.
[Bologna or Venice], MDXLI [1541].

Another edition.
Colophon: Stampata in Venegia per Giovanni Andrea Vavassore...
M.D.XXXXIII [1543].

An imitation of Erasmus's *Praise of Folly*, this encomium to madness includes a passage lauding the natives of the West Indies for their disregard of material things. They are compared with the citizens of Plato's *Republic* who care nothing for gold and silver and share property in common. Albergati draws upon the descriptions of American natives by Columbus and Vespucci. But his idealization of them as Noble Savages is new and comes earlier than scholars have previously believed this to have occurred.

1541 edition acquired 1975. Associates of the John Carter Brown Library.
1543 edition acquired 1976. Louisa Dexter Sharpe Metcalf Fund.

25 DOMENICO MELLINI, CA. 1540 – CA. 1610
Descrizione Dell'Entrata Della sereniss. Reina Giovanna d'Austria.
In Fiorenza appresso i Giunti MDLXVI [1566].

America represented an exotic land from which came strange animals, new plants, people in wild costumes. As Giovanna d'Austria, engaged to marry the Grand Duke of Tuscany, Francesco de' Medici, entered Florence in 1566, her procession passed through streets lined with symbolic decoration—a stationary "parade" through which she and her party moved as spectators. She entered the western gates (Porto Prato) and soon encountered men costumed as the great figures of the Florentine past, among whom were Amerigo Vespucci and Paolo del Pozzo Toscanelli. Later, as she passed the Spini palace, there was a huge painting depicting Peru, an allegorical representation containing nymphs, putti, birds, and exotic American animals. As the painting has apparently not survived, the only record of its appearance is in this verbal description of it.

Sabin 47453.
Acquired 1976. Endowment funds.

V *Italian Historians of the Great Explorations*

INFORMATION about the New World reached Italy in many ways: through travelers' stories, personal letters, reports by merchants, dispatches of Italian ambassadors to European courts (and of their spies), reports of missionaries to their superiors. The first writers to assimilate the information on America and to present it to the public were Italians.

ITALIAN EYEWITNESS REPORTS OF EXPLORATION AND CONQUEST

The letters of Columbus and Vespucci are the best-known Italian personal narratives of the discovery period but by no means the only ones. Besides the three described below, this catalogue also contains the account of Verrazzano found in Ramusio's 1556 collection of voyages (number 32).

26 [ANTONIO PIGAFETTA], CA. 1480/91 – CA. 1534
Le voyage et navigation faict par les Espaignolz es Isles de Mollucques....
On les vend a Paris en la maison de Simon de Colines ... [1525].

The only contemporary printed account of Magellan's voyage around the world by a participant was written by a nobleman of Vicenza, Antonio Pigafetta. Pigafetta, "prompted by a craving for experience and glory," as he said of himself, joined the fleet that sailed from Seville in August of 1519. He was aboard Magellan's flagship *Trinidad*, and was one of the few survivors of that difficult first circumnavigation. Upon his return, Pigafetta informs us, he presented Charles V, who had sponsored the expedition, a copy of his diary (now lost). He then went to Lisbon, where he presented King João with a manuscript, and then on to Paris where he offered another manuscript to Marie Louise, regent and mother of Francis I. Neither of these versions is known.

Pigafetta wrote his book in Italy in 1524. In 1525 he visited the court of the French King, and his lively, gossipy account of the voyage was published in French translation that year. This helped to stimulate royal support of Verrazzano's project which was intended to achieve a similar result—to find a trade route to the East Indies by a northwesterly route, Spain and Portugal having laid claim to routes by the southwest and southeast.

Plate VI.

JCB(3)1:95; JCB *Collection's Progress* 20; Harrisse (BAV) 134; James A. Robertson's edition and translation, Cleveland, 1906, is still considered the best text.
Acquired before 1856 by John Carter Brown.

27 NICOLAO DE ALBENINO, B. 1514
Verdadera relacion: de lo sussedido enlos Reynos e provincias d'l peru, dẽde la yda ellos d'l vi Rey Blasco nuñes vela, hasta el desbarato y muerte de gonçalo Piçarro.
Colophon: ... Seville [2 January] M.D. xlix [1549]. En casa da Juan de Leon.

Nicolao de Albenino was a Florentine, born about 1514, who is presumed to have gone to Peru in 1535. During the next forty years he was one of a large number of Italians who were employed in the great silver mines of Potosí, and he eventually rose to a position of considerable responsibility.

This book is the earliest account of the Gonzalo Pizarro rebellion of 1544–1548. Albenino played a role in the turbulence as a loyalist to the Spanish crown. His was the only account by a participant and eyewitness to the rebellion to be published at the time, and it is still an important source for that important incident which tested Spain's ability to rule its distant colonies. Only one other copy of this book is known—in Paris at the Bibliothèque Nationale.

JCBAR 39:2–8.
Obtained 1939. The gift of Mrs. Jesse H. Metcalf.

ITALIANS AS HISTORIANS OF AMERICA

The first author to assimilate the information concerning the discoveries was Italian, as were the editors of the first collections of explorers' accounts and of the first list of books on America. The texts of Peter Martyr and Ramusio had wide circulation—the former and large portions of the latter were even translated into English.

28 GIROLAMO BENZONI, b. 1519
La Historia Del Mondo Nuovo Di M. Girolamo Benzoni Milanese. . . .
Colophon: In Venetia, Appresso Francesco Rampazetto. MDLXV [1565].

Benzoni, born of a poor Milanese family, went to America as a young soldier in 1541. He served in the Spanish army for fourteen years in such varied posts as Haiti, Cuba, Panama, Colombia, and Peru. His narrative reflects the hard conditions of his service: it is rough and ill-written but vivid in its details, conveying with great fidelity the dangers and deprivations of an ordinary soldier. There was no room for flattery in such a book, and Spaniards were upset by the harsh portrayal of their colonies which Benzoni presented. Benzoni's book was reprinted many times, often as anti-Spanish propaganda, and it played an important role in creating "the black legend," the negative impression of Spanish rule held by many.

JCB(3)1:226–227; Sabin 4790.
Acquired ca. 1847 by John Carter Brown.

29 FRANCANZANO DA MONTALBODDO
. . . Paesi Novamente retrovati. . . .
Colophon: Stampato in Vicentia . . . Henrico Vicentino . . . M.CCCCVii [1507].

This is the first printed collection of voyages and travels of the Age of Discovery. It includes the first printed appearance of Cà da Mosto's travels to Africa as well as reprints of accounts of Columbus's first three voyages and Vespucci's "third voyage." It was translated into Latin, German, and French within a few years and was read throughout Europe. It is believed that more people learned the news of the discoveries in both America and Asia from this book than from any other.

Plate VII.

JCB(3)1:43; Harrisse (BAV) 48; Church 25; Penrose, *Travel and Discovery*, p. 277.
Acquired 1849 by John Carter Brown.

30 PIETRO MARTIRE D'ANGHIERA, 1457–1526
Opera.
Colophon: Impressum Hispali [Seville] cum summa diligencia per Jacobum corumberger. [1511.]

Peter Martyr (to give his Anglicized name), the first historian of America, was born at Arona on the shores of Lago Maggiore. In 1494 he was ordained and in the same year was appointed tutor to the children of

Ferdinand and Isabella. He was a friend of Columbus, Vasco da Gama, Cortés, Magellan, Cabot, and Vespucci, and, from conversations with these men as well as from his position as a member of the Council for the Indies, he was able to get accurate reports. He had started to prepare a history of the discovery of the Indies as early as 1494. Samuel Eliot Morison wrote of Peter Martyr, "The value of Peter Martyr's letters and of his Decades is very great for he had a keen and critical intelligence which pierced some of the cosmographical fancies of Columbus ... and he gives us more information about the second Voyage than any other contemporary historian."

JCB(3)1:52; Harrisse (BAV) 66, additions 41; *World Encompassed* 52, plate XVII.
Acquired 1846 by John Carter Brown.

31 GIOVANNI BATTISTA RAMUSIO, 1485–1557 (EDITOR)
Summario De La Generale Historia De L'Indie Occidentali....
[Venice, October 1534.]

Ramusio, a Venetian, edited the second collection of texts (after Montalboddo's in 1507) on America. He published three texts: two lengthy histories of recent explorations by Peter Martyr and Fernández de Oviedo, and a third short piece, a translation of a first-hand anonymous account of newly discovered Peru, *La conquista del Peru*, which had appeared at Seville in 1534. Not as extensive as Montalboddo's *Paesi novamente retrovati* or his own great *Navigationi e viaggi*, the work served to provide Italians with accurate information at a time when explorers were learning the dimensions of the two continents.

The map which was apparently intended to accompany this volume is described at number 103.

JCB(3)1:114; Harrisse (BAV) 190; Church 69.
Acquired 1846 by John Carter Brown.

32 GIOVANNI BATTISTA RAMUSIO, 1485–1557
Terzo Volume Delle Navigationi Et Viaggi Nel Quale Si Contengono Le Navigatione al Mondo Nuovo....
In Venetia Nella Stamperia De Giunti. L'Anno MDLVI [1556].

Nearly twenty years after publishing his *Summario historia de l'Indie*, Ramusio began a massive publishing project: he assembled texts of discovery and exploration in three thick folio volumes, each one devoted to a continent. The third volume, the one on America, contains, among many basic documents, the first printed report of the voyages of Giovanni da Verrazzano. The map "La Nuova Francia," executed in woodcut by Giacomo Gastaldi, accompanied the Verrazzano text. It represents the coast from New York Bay to Labrador—Verrazzano's "Port du Refuge" is Narragansett Bay.

Plate VIII.

JCB(3)1:194; George B. Parks "The contents and sources of Ramusio's Navigationi," *Bulletin of the New York Public Library*, 59, 6, June 1955, pp. 279–313; Wroth, *Verrazzano*, pp. 205–209.
Acquired before 1854 by John Carter Brown.

33 ANTONIO POSSEVINO, 1534–1611
Apparato All' Historia Di tutte le Nationi. Et Il Modo Di Studiare La Geografia. . . .
In Venetia, Presso Gio. Battista Coitti Senese . . . 1598.

Italian Jesuits organized materials for instruction in their schools in clear, tightly structured ways that looked forward to modern pedagogy. In this handbook for advanced students of history in Jesuit schools, the learned Jesuit Antonio Possevino included a chapter entitled "Historici delle cose dell'India." This appears to be the first extensive list of books relating to America. Most of the works are easily identifiable, and many can be found in the John Carter Brown Library. Some of the books cited, such as Ferdinand Colombo's life of his father and Lorenzo Gambara's poem about Columbus, are included in this catalogue.

Backer 6:1079–80.
Acquired 1968. Louisa Dexter Sharpe Metcalf Fund.

ITALY AS A CHANNEL OF INFORMATION

News tended to gravitate to Italy during the fifteenth century, and Italy was a conduit through which much of the news of America passed to the rest of Europe. Northern Europeans often learned of Spanish activities through Italian translations such as the early account of the conquest of Peru which follows.

34 [ANTONIO DE OLAVE]
Passio gloriosi martyris beati patris fratris Andree de Spoleto. . . .
Colophon: Impressum Bononiae per Justinianum Ruberieñ. Anno.
M.D. xxxii die iii Junii. . . . [3 June 1532.]

The conquest of the Mayan people of the Yucatan peninsula began in 1527, and resistance was so determined that large sections were brought under Spanish control only in 1697. This pamphlet includes two letters, dated Mexico, 6 June 1531, by Martín de Valencia and Juan de Zumárraga, Franciscan missionaries in Yucatan, as well as a letter on the martyrdom of another Franciscan, Andrea da Spoleto, in Africa. The pamphlet is reprinted from an edition of the letters printed at Toulouse in April 1532, where a French translation was also published. The edition printed at Bologna was unrecorded before the Library obtained this copy of it.

Acquired 1976. Associates of the John Carter Brown Library.

35 [FRANCISCO DE XEREZ], B. 1500
Libro Primo De La Conquista del Peru & provincia del Cuzco de le Indie occidentali.
Colophon: Stampato in Vinegia per Maestro Stephano da Sabio del MDXXXV [1535]. . . .

Francisco de Xerez, Francisco Pizarro's secretary, departed from Spain with his employer in 1530. He participated in the decisive early stages of the conquistador's campaign. After he had murdered the Inca ruler Atahualpa, Pizarro, who was illiterate but no fool, ordered his secretary to write an account of the conquest, accentuating the heroism and boldness, and to get back to Spain with the story fast. By accompanying the first gold shipment home Xerez could blunt reaction against the cruel, deceitful manner of conquest by his words and by lucre. The *Verdadera relacion* was published in Seville in July 1534. It was translated for a Venetian audience and published in March the next year. This is a longer and more detailed account than the first account of Peru published by Ramusio a few months earlier.

JCB(3)1:119; Harrisse (BAV) 201; Church 73; Sabin 105721.
Acquired 1846 by John Carter Brown.

36   JESUITS
Avisi Particolari delle Indie di Portugallo.
In Roma per Valerio Dorico & Luigi Fratelli Bressani . . . 1552.

The Society of Jesus was authorized in 1540, and in 1542 its first missionary, St. Francis Xavier, went out to India. The first mission to America was Father Nombrega and five companions who went to Brazil in 1549. St. Ignatius Loyola organized the order as a military "company." In order to maintain high standards and rigid discipline, organization was essential, particularly as the Society's missions were so widely dispersed. To exercise control Loyola had each missionary report to regional supervisors and send information on the lands in which they were stationed. He wrote: ". . . if there are other things that may seem extraordinary, let them be noted, for instance, details about animals and plants that either are not known at all, or not of such a size, etc. And this news—sauce for the taste of a certain curiosity that is not evil and is wont to be found among men—may come in the same letters or in other letters separately." The reports were edited in Rome and Loyola quickly realized that they would have wide appeal. In 1552 the Society began to publish them regularly. In this first Jesuit letter there is a report from the new and struggling mission to Brazil.

JCB(3)1:166; Streit 2:1221, 4:669; *Europe Informed*, pp. 107–108.
Acquired 1846 by John Carter Brown.

VI   *The Reputation of Columbus in Italy*

COLUMBUS'S reputation, at first eclipsed by the fame of Vespucci, steadily improved once it was realized that the Indies of Columbus were Vespucci's *Mundus Novus*. Fifty years after his death Columbus was recognized as a hero. The following works represent some of the stages of his elevation.

37   RAFFAELE MAFFEI, OF VOLTERRA, 1451–1522
   . . . *Commentariorum Urbanorum.* . . .
   Colophon: ac Impressus Romae per Ioannem Besicken . . . MDVI [1506].

This book is a general encyclopaedia which contains a chapter, "Loca nuper reperta," on Columbus's discoveries. It is the first book of a general nature which included information about Columbus; it appeared the year of his death, 1506.

Harrisse (BAV) additions 22; Sabin 43763.
Acquired 1971. Benefactors of the John Carter Brown Library.

38 BIBLE. PSALMS

Psalterum, Hebreum, Grecum, Arabicum, & Chaldeum cum tribus latinis interpretatoinibus [sic.] *& glossis.*

Colophon: [Genoa], Impressit Petrus Paulus Porrus. . . . [1516.]

This psalter in five languages is the first polyglot liturgical work ever printed. The editor, Agostino Giustiniani, Bishop of Nebbio, included a paragraph on Columbus as a note to Psalm xix, 4. This note is the first published claim by the city of Genoa to the man who was to become its most famous son. The Library has two copies of the beautifully printed psalter; this one is on vellum.

JCB (3)1:64; Harrisse (BAV) 88; Sabin 66468.
Acquired before 1865 by John Carter Brown.

39 FERNANDO COLÓN, 1488–1539

Historie De S. D. Fernando Colombo; Nelle quali s'ha particolare, & vera relatione della vita, & de' fatti dell'Ammiraglio D. Christoforo Colombo, Suo padre. . . .

In Venetia, MDLXXI [1571]. Appresso Francesco de' Franceschi Sanese.

Fernando Colón was Columbus's illegitimate son. He was brought up as a royal page and became wealthy enough to form a library of 15,000 volumes. He saw his father brought home in chains, went with him on the fourth voyage, and dedicated his own life to writing a biography to vindicate him. His completed manuscript (now lost) found its way to Italy, and this book was the first appearance of this important source for the Discoverer's life.

JCB (1)3:244; Church 114; Sabin 14674.
Acquired 1846 by John Carter Brown.

40 PAOLO GIOVIO, 1483–1552

. . . Elogia virorum bellica virtute illustrium veris imaginibus supposita, quae apud Musaeum spectantur. . . .

Florentiae In Officium Laurentii Torentini . . . MDLI [1551].

One of the significant measures of the rise of Columbus's reputation was his inclusion in this collection of military men. Paolo Giovio, Bishop of Nocera, gathered portraits of heroes of the past, including Romulus and Alexander the Great, as well as of the leaders of his time, among whom was Cortés. He installed them in his private museum on Lake Como. Among the portraits of recent heroes was one of Columbus. In this book the Bishop described the paintings in his collection. The Library also possesses the Italian translations of this book.

Acquired 1925. Endowment funds.

41 PAOLO GIOVIO, 1483–1552
... *Elogia virorum bellica virtute illustrium*. ...
Basileae. M.D.LXXI [1571].

This Basel 1571 edition of Giovio's book on military leaders is the first that contains woodcut copies of the oil paintings in Giovio's collection. The likeness of the woodcut of Columbus is not authentic, but it is the first published portrait of Columbus and influenced later pictures of him. The significance of its appearance is that the likeness was considered of sufficient importance to collect and to publish in the third quarter of the sixteenth century. This copy of the book belonged to John Evelyn, the English "virtuoso" (1620–1706), whose library was recently dispersed at auction.

Acquired 1978. Louisa Dexter Sharpe Metcalf Fund.

COLUMBUS AS A THEME IN CINQUECENTO ITALIAN POETRY

It took several generations to gain the perspective to appreciate the significance of Columbus and his discoveries and still longer for them to be celebrated in verse. Leicester Bradner, now Professor of English Emeritus at Brown University, has studied sixteenth-century Latin poems using Columbus as a theme.

42 LORENZO GAMBARA, 1506–1596
... *De navigatione Christophori Columbi libri quattuor*.
Romae, Apud Franciscum Zannettum, MDLXXXI [1581].

In 1536 a courtier to Charles V suggested to young Gambara that he treat the discovery of America in poetry. Not one to be rushed, Gambara set out forty-five years later to write an historical poem. He used Peter Martyr and other original sources for his information, adhered closely to historical fact, and eschewed the traditional devices of epic poetry: there are no long speeches, no catalogues of ships, no supernatural machinery. The poem was well received, as indicated by the fact that it was reprinted in 1583 and 1585.

JCB (3)1:286; Sabin 26500; Leicester Bradner, "Columbus in Sixteenth-Century Poetry," in *Essays Honoring Lawrence C. Wroth*, Portland, Maine, 1951, pp. 16–19.
Acquired 1836 by John Carter Brown.

43 GIULIO CESARE STELLA, 1564–1624
... *Columbeidos Libri Priores Duo*. ...
Romae, Apud Sanctium, & Soc. MD.XC. [1590].

The poets following Gambara who used Columbus as a theme altered fact to make their stories attractive. This Latin poem is modeled upon Tasso's *La Gerusalemme liberata* and its main theme is Satan's opposition to the conversion of the heathen. In order to stop Columbus, Satan disguises himself as an Officer of the Fleet and proceeds to incite a mutiny. God sees this and sends an angel to warn Columbus in a dream, and the voyage continues in this fantastic manner. Stella completed only two books of his projected epic, but they stimulated other poets to use the voyage of Columbus as an epic theme.

JCB (3)1:324; Sabin 91217; Leicester Bradner, *op. cit.*, pp. 19–23.
Acquired 1846 by John Carter Brown.

44   GIOVANNI GIORGINI, D. 1606

Il Mondo Nuovo. . . .
In Iesi Appresso Pietro Farri, M.D.XCVI [1596].

This epic poem of twenty-four cantos is written in *ottava rima* stanzas in the style of Ariosto's *Orlando Furioso*. It is full of supernatural events and romantic incidents and has little regard for historical fact. In this version King Ferdinand of Spain accompanies Columbus on his second voyage and then conquers Mexico with a slight assist from Cortés. Although overshadowed by the King, Columbus appears with the conventional virtues of a perfect courtier: he is pious, learned, brave, wise, loyal.

JCB (3)1:342; Sabin 27473; Leicester Bradner, *op. cit.*, pp. 23–27.
Acquired 1846 by John Carter Brown.

45   TOMASO STIGLIANI, 1573–1651

Del Mondo Nuovo. . . .
In Piacenza per Allesandro Bazacchi, 1617.

A native of Matera in Basilicata, Stigliani grew up in Naples where he knew the poet Marino and, possibly, Tasso. These were the great poets of his time, the ones admired in courtly circles, and he emulated them, as well as Ariosto, in this bid for poetic glory. Stigliani used Columbus and the discovery of America as a framework of reality in which to tell fanciful stories of fictional characters in exotic settings. Instead of achieving glory, he was severely criticized for his excesses by contemporary poets, including Marino himself and Angelico Aprosio.

JCB (3)1:122; Sabin 91728.
Acquired 1869 by John Carter Brown.

VII   *Vespucci as a Theme in Cinquecento Italian Poetry*

VESPUCCI'S reputation in the sixteenth century declined as Columbus's rose. There was no biography of him written then—none in fact until Angelo Maria Bandini published *Vita e lettere* at Florence in 1745. In such works as Leandro Alberti's *Descrittione Di Tutta Italia* (the Library has the first edition, Bologna, 1550) the man who is known above all for his first name is mentioned as the prominent Florentine Alberigo Vespucci. Florentines were most concerned with the memory of Vespucci. The following group of poems are all by Florentines; Bandini and Stanislao Canovai, who took up Amerigo's cause in the eighteenth century, were Florentine as well.

46   GIOVANNI BATTISTA STROZZI, 1551–1634
[First canto of a poem on Amerigo Vespucci, in 93 octaves.]
[Manuscript, Florence, before 1601.]

This is the first known poem to use Amerigo Vespucci as a subject. It is the first canto—possibly the only one ever completed—by a poet active in Florentine literary circles at the end of the sixteenth century. The poem's existence was known because of early references to it by Strozzi's literary friends. A distant relative in the eighteenth century believed that there was a copy in the Magliabecchi Collection, which became part of the National Library in Florence, but the copy is no longer there. This manuscript, probably a contemporary secretarial copy, seems to be the sole copy still extant.

A. S. Barbi, *Un Accademico Mercante e Poeta*, Firenze, 1900; the poem is published by Professor Franco Fido in the *Stanford Italian Review*, number 2, September 1979.
Acquired 1977. Obtained with a gift from Mrs. Marion Brewington and funds from the Benefactors of the John Carter Brown Library.

47   RAFFAELO GUALTEROTTI, 1543–1638
L'America Di Raffael' Gualterotti Dedicata Al Sereniss. Don Cosimo Medici II. . . .
In Firenze, Appresso Cosimo Giunti, 1611.

This is the first canto of an epic poem on Vespucci. Gualterotti, a minor painter as well as a minor poet, presented it as a sample to Cosimo Medici II, Grand Duke of Tuscany, and offered to show him the remainder of the poem if the first canto was received with favor. Medici patronage was not forthcoming, and only this first canto—the "prospectus"—was ever printed. What happened to the manuscript of the other cantos, if, indeed, they were ever written, is not known. This is the earliest known printed poem on Vespucci, and because of the circumstances of its publication, it is very rare.

JCB(3)2:75; Sabin 29050.
Acquired in 1846 by John Carter Brown.

48   GIROLAMO BARTOLOMMÉI SMEDUCCI, 1584?–1662
L'America Poema Eroico. . . .
In Roma, MDCL [1650]. Nella Stamperia di Ludovico Grignani.

A Florentine poet, lawyer, member of the Accademia della Crusca, Bartolomméi Smeducci intended to write a new *Odyssey*, in imitation of Homer, but elevated through an understanding of Aristotle. The voyage of Amerigo Vespucci is given allegorical significance, ample classical decoration, and considerable length: there are 560 folio pages of double columns of verse.

JCB(3)1:343–394; Sabin 3797; *Dizionario Biografico degli Italiani*, Rome, 1977, vol. 6, p. 789; Gamba 1782.
Acquired 1846 by John Carter Brown.

VIII *Italian Physicians and America*

THE discovery of America had significant medical ramifications. New diseases were encountered here, although Europeans, hardened by over a century of bouts with the plague, carried with them many more to America. Oceanic travel presented health hazards and spread diseases across the seas. New medicinal plants were found in America and helped solve some medical problems. Italian physicians were involved in solving some of the problems and disseminated some of the medicines. This is to be expected as Italian medical schools, traditionally the best in Europe, made enormous contributions to advances in the whole range of medical science during the period 1500–1800. The following section is a sampling with two books on an American disease, syphilis, and two on an American medicine, quinine.

49.

49 ANONYMOUS

Capitulo over recetta delo arbore over Legno detto Guaiana [sic]: Remedio contra el male Gallico.

Colophon: [Venice], per Alexandrum de Bindonis. 1520.

Columbus's companions of his first voyage brought back with them a virulent form of syphilis. The disease swept swiftly throughout Europe: it was the first way in which America influenced the lives of those in the Old World. Cures were desperately sought. The first medicine for syphilis was the bark of the guaiac tree of the West Indies, a cure learned from the Indians. Thus, guaiac bark was the first botanical gift to the Old World. This is an early description of guaiac bark. The book is unrecorded in bibliographies of Americana or of medicine.

Francisco Guerra, "The Problem of Syphilis," in *First Images of America: The Impact of the New World on the Old*, Los Angeles, 1976, vol. 2, pp. 845–851.

Acquired 1968. Lathrop Colgate Harper Fund.

50 GIROLAMO FRACASTORO, 1483–1553

... Syphilis Sive Morbus Gallicus. ...

Veronae, MDXXX [1530].

The name of the disease originally called "the French Disease" was changed to syphilis after the protagonist of this Latin poem. In the poem a shepherd, Syphilis, is imagined to be the first sufferer from the malady. Girolamo Fracastoro, a physician, astronomer, and man of letters of Verona, uses the story of the shepherd to describe the symptoms and offer means of treatment for the disease. He was the first to recognize it as being a venereal disease, thus making this a substantial medical as well as literary contribution.

JCB(3)1:100; Harrisse (BAV) additions 91.
Acquired 1906. Endowment funds.

51 SEBASTIANO BADO, FL. 1640–1676

Anastasis Corticis Peruviae, Seu Chinae Chinae Defensio. ...

Genuae [Genoa], Typis Joannis Calenzani, M.DC.LXIII [1663].

Chinchona bark which contains quinine was first used by Indians of the jungles of Ecuador, Peru, and Chile to treat malaria. Missionaries learned of it in the 1630's, and by 1650 Roman Jesuits were encouraging its use. Chinchona was popularly called "Jesuit Bark," and it was taken as a patent medicine for all fevers.

Sebastiano Bado, a Genoese physician who specialized in sanitation and public health, was a strong believer in the effectiveness of chinchona. He was one of the first reputable medical doctors to support its use, and his book is one of the first to examine the bark scientifically.

Garrison-Morton 1826; Edward John Waring, *Bibliotheca therapeutica*, London, 1878–1879, 338.
Acquired 1968. Louisa Dexter Sharpe Metcalf Fund.

52 FRANCESCO TORTI, 1658–1741

Therapeutice Specialis Ad Febres quasdam Perniciosas....

... Mutinae, [Modena], MDCCXII [1712]. Typis Bartholomaei Soliani....

Before Torti's work appeared quinine was used to treat all fevers. The frequent failure of quinine cast doubts upon its effectiveness. Torti, who isolated and named malaria, recognized that quinine was appropriate only for the cure of malarial fever. This book represents a milestone in man's conquest of a disease that has killed millions.

Garrison–Morton 5231.
Acquired 1968. Associates of the John Carter Brown Library.

IX Italian Missionaries on the Frontiers of Seventeenth-Century America

THE seventeenth century was a period of consolidation, growth, and expansion for the missionary orders. By this time they had reached to all parts of Spanish, Portuguese, and French America. Italians were involved as missionaries in all orders and in all regions, and their work and writings are an important legacy.

Information about frontier areas from non-Italian missionaries often appeared first in Rome because, as the place where the orders' headquarters were located, reports of activities were sent there regularly.

53 EUSEBIO FRANCISCO KINO, CA. 1645–1711

Passage Par Terre A La California Decouvert par le Rev. Père Eusebe-François Kino Jesuite depuis 1698 jusqu'a 1701....

Engraved map, 21×26 cm., from *Lettres Edifiantes Et Curieuses, Ecrites Des Missions ... de la Compagnie de Jésus. V. Recueil.*

A Paris, Chez Nicolas Le Clerc ... M.DCCV [1705].

The Jesuit Father Kino founded a score of missions which are now Arizona towns. Born at Segno, near Trento in Italy, Kino had hoped to join the mission in China but was sent to the Spanish frontier in northern Mexico. He used his considerable mathematical skills to map large areas of what is now the southwestern United States. Kino supervised the establishment of missions in Baja California and organized an overland supply system for them. He soon realized that the old maps of the area were drastically incorrect, so he prepared a new one. His map of Baja California, first included in a collection of letters from Jesuit missions, finally put to rest the notion that California was an island. The hispanicized form of his name is now used rather than the Italian Chino.

Ernest J. Burrus, *Kino and the Cartography of Northwestern New Spain*, Tucson, 1965.
Acquired 1957. Associates of the John Carter Brown Library.

54 FRANCESCO GIUSEPPE BRESSANI, 1612–1672
Breve Relatione D'Alcune Missioni De' PP. della Compagnia di Giesù nella Nuova Francia....
In Macerata, Per gli Heredi d'Agostino Grisei. 1653.

Between 1642 and 1651, Bressani, a native of Rome, served as a Jesuit missionary in Canada. The first two years were spent in learning Indian language and customs; then he requested permission to proselytize among the most distant Hurons. He was captured by the Iroquois, was cruelly tortured, sold to a Dutch trader, and returned to Europe. Undaunted, he returned to Quebec in 1645 and for seven years worked among the Hurons, who were constantly attacked by Iroquois. When the Hurons were driven from their lands, the order returned some of the missionaries to Europe. Among them was Bressani, who recorded his experiences during the turbulent early years of French Canada.

Plate IX.

JCB(3)2:428; Sabin 77734; Streit 2:2585.
Acquired 1846 by John Carter Brown.

55 ALONSO DE OVALLE, 1601–1651
Historica Relacion Del Reyno de Chile....
En Roma, por Francisco Cavallo. M.DC.XLVI [1646].
Engraved map of Chile, 58×117 cm.

This work, the first general history of Chile, was written in part to encourage missionaries to come to the Spanish frontier, and was published in Rome simultaneously in Italian and Spanish. Our second copy of the Spanish-language edition, originally in the Huth collection, contains a large engraved map of Chile. This detailed map, known only in this copy and one in Paris, was the fullest record of the southwest coast of South America at the time, and the source of maps of the area for a century. This is a striking example of the kind of important information that missions sent to Rome and that was first published there.

JCB(3)2:345; Lawrence C. Wroth, "Alonso de Ovalle's Large Map of Chile, 1646," in *Imago Mundi*, XIV (1959), pp. 90–95.
Acquired 1917. Endowment funds.

56 DIONIGI CARLI, CA. 1637–1695
Viaggio Del P. Dionigi de Carli da Piacenza, e del P. Michel Angel de' Guatini.
Reggio, per Prospero Vedrotti, 1671.

Michel Angelo de Gualtini and Dionigi Carli were Capuchin missionaries sent to the Congo. Because they stayed at Pernambuco in Brazil on their way to Africa (their description of Recife after the expulsion of the Dutch is the second known account) and because they witnessed, and opposed, the slave trade, they are important sources for Brazilian history. Other Italian Capuchins sent to the Congo—Cavazzi da Montecuccolo, Merolla da Sorrento, and Zucchelli da Gradisca—are also important historians of Brazil and the Congo.

Streit 16:4486; cf. Borba de Moraes 1:131.
Acquired 1969. Associates of the John Carter Brown Library.

X The Seventeenth Century

DURING the seventeenth century there were no startling discoveries of unexpected new lands, new peoples, or new wealth to catch the attention of Italians as in the previous century. Italy itself was caught up in problems of its own. Furthermore, access to America was controlled by the enormous power of Spain. As a result there are fewer books, certainly fewer which contain direct, accurate, and important news from America, printed in Italy during this century than in the sixteenth century. Nevertheless when opportunity presented itself, there were enterprizing individuals who seized it.

57 FRANCESCO CARLETTI, 1573?–1636
Ragionamenti....
In Firenze Nel Garbo, Nella Stamperìa di Giuseppe Manni, 1701.

Francesco Carletti was born in Florence, probably in 1573. At the age of eighteen he was sent to Seville to learn the intricacies of international maritime trade. He set out from Spain in 1594 on a trading voyage that by 1602 had lengthened into a circumnavigation of the globe. Dutch privateers in the Atlantic deprived him of the profits of his travels, and he returned home to Florence richer only in experience. Observant and articulate, his reports were welcomed by Ferdinando de' Medici to whom Carletti presented a manuscript. His reports were published almost a century later—in 1701.

JCB (1)3:5; Sabin 10908; there is a modern edition, edited by Gianfranco Silvestro, Torino, Einaudi [1958]. Acquired 1865 by John Carter Brown.

58 ABRAHAM NICOLAS AMELOT DE LA HOUSSAYE, 1634–1706
La Storia Del Governo Di Venezia....
In Colonia [i.e., Paris], Appresso Pietro del Martello. M.DC.LXXXI [1681].

Some Italians of the seventeenth century blamed the discovery of America for the decline of the Italian states in the order of international powers. Amelot de la Houssaye, writer and translator, born at Orléans, France, served as secretary to the ambassador to Venice and was in a position to examine the Venetian state closely. Venice had slipped badly both in its political effectiveness and its economic strength since 1492. In this book on the history of the government of Venice first published at Paris in 1676–1677, Amelot refers to the damage to Venetian commerce caused by competing imports from America.

Acquired 1968. Associates of the John Carter Brown Library.

59 GIORGIO PONZA
La Science De L'Homme De Qualité, Ou L'Idée Générale De la Cosmographie....
Turin M.DC.LXXXIV [1684]. Par les Héritiers Ianelli.

In this handbook on the geography and history which every gentleman should know there are a few pages on America. The author, however, obviously regarded information about America of little consequence:

[51]

in this book New Amsterdam, which twenty years before had passed to the English and been renamed New York, is still listed as a Dutch colony! Further research and further collecting may alter our view, but it seems that this accurately reflects the limits of seventeenth-century knowledge of America.

Acquired 1971. The gift of Mr. and Mrs. Samuel J. Hough in memory of Lawrence C. Wroth.

60 LOUIS HENNEPIN, CA. 1640 – CA. 1705
Descrizione Della Luigiana; Paese nuovamente scoperto nell' America Settentrionale. . . .
In Bologna, per Giacomo Monti. 1686.

Hennepin, Recollect brother, explorer, teller of tall tales, accompanied LaSalle on his 1678 exploration of the Mississippi. This book, a translation of his *Description de la Louisiane*, first published at Paris, 1683, is regarded as an accurate account of LaSalle's expedition. Hennepin's later writing was more fanciful: it seems that in order to match the success of this book he decided to invent further adventures. This is the first book in Italian describing the Midwest of the United States.

Plate X.

JCB (1675–1700) 165; Sabin 31356; Streit 2:2732.
Acquired 1847 by John Carter Brown.

61 [CONTE VALERIO ZANI] D. 1696
Il Genio Vagante Biblioteca curiosa Di cento e più Relazioni Di Viaggi Stranieri de' nostri tempi. . . .
In Parma, per Giuseppe dell Oglio & Ippolito Rasati MDCXCI[–MDCXCIII] [1691–1693]. Four volumes.

The great Italian collections of voyages by Montalboddo and Ramusio (numbers 29 and 32) are imitated in this small, cramped, anonymously published work. The account of the French explorations in the Mississippi Valley, the vast region labeled "Luigiana," is an abridged version of the Bologna, 1686, Italian translation of Hennepin. As modest as this publication is, it did bring together many texts of more recent explorations which would have otherwise not been available to Italian readers.

JCB (1675–1700) 250–251; Streit 1:715.
Acquired 1969. Associates of the John Carter Brown Library.

62 GIOVANNI FRANCESCO GEMELLI CARERI
Giro Del Mondo. . . .
Venezia, MDCCXIX [1719]. Presso Sebastiano Coletti. Nine volumes.

Gemelli Careri is a mysterious figure. For many years scholars thought that his voyage was fictional and that his work was written in an armchair, copying other books. But his observations have been verified over the centuries, and his voyage is now accepted as factual. His world travels were first published at Naples in nine volumes in 1699.

Gemelli Careri sought out historical materials about the places he visited and his sixth volume, which deals with Mexico, contains information taken from pre-conquest codices. Among the illustrations are Aztec warriors derived from such a manuscript. There are ample passages on natural history: in this volume vanilla and cacao, both plants native to America, are among those illustrated. He also described the life and economy of the areas he visited, and in this volume there is an illustration of a Mexican silver mine.

JCBAR 21:7.
Acquired 1920. Endowment funds.

XI *Italian Erudition and the Preservation of American Artifacts*

THE role of early Italian scholars and collectors in preserving the manuscripts and artifacts of American Indian cultures is not appreciated, yet without these acts of preservation the study by later generations would have been impossible.

Throughout the period 1500–1800 Italian collectors continued the great tradition established in previous centuries of forming private collections of objects. The Medici, Grand Dukes of Tuscany, formed extensive collections of paintings, precious stones, scientific instruments, stuffed animals, and manuscripts, which are the basis of several national museums. A recent study by Detlef Heikamp, *Mexico and the Medici*, Florence, 1972, reveals the extent of the Medici collections in one area. Heikamp also contributed an article on our theme, "American Objects in Italian Collections of the Renaissance and Baroque: A Survey," to the book *First Images in America*.

63 VINCENZO CARTARI, 1531 – CA. 1570
Seconda Novissima Editione Delle Imagini De Gli Dei Delli Antichi....
In Padova. Nella stamperia di Pietro Paolo Tozzi. M.DC.XXVI [1626].

Cartari was born in Reggio Emilia, probably in 1531. His life was spent in service to the Estes, Dukes of Ferrara, who patronized arts and learning. When Cartari first published his *Imagini de i Dei* in 1556 he was concerned with the images of gods in Classical Antiquity and the Near East. In this posthumous edition the editor, Lorenzo Pignoria, added images from Asia and America in expanding the work. The images of Aztec gods are taken from a manuscript in the Vatican library. Some of the early missionaries destroyed many idolatrous Mexican manuscripts in order to eradicate the Aztec religion, but, as the Church's position became secure, many others were saved. It was thus that the great library at the Vatican became a depository of many important Aztec codices.

JCB (3)2:198–99; Sabin 11105; there is a good biography of Cartari by M. Palma in the *Dizionario Biografico degli Italiani*, Rome, 1977, vol. 20, pp. 793–796.
Acquired 1910. The gift of William E. Foster.

64 LODOVICO MOSCARDO
Note Overo Memorie Del Museo Di Lodovico Moscardo Nobile Veronese....
In Padova, MDCLVI [1656]. Per Paolo Frambotto.

Moscardo's "cabinet" or museum of natural history and archaeological finds was one of the principal collections of rarities of its day. Among the objects from America listed in this annotated catalogue of the Collection is a pair of Aztec slippers made with great skill. Many American-Indian pieces now in public museums were preserved in the private "cabinets" of this kind.

Acquired 1973. Lathrop Colgate Harper Fund.

65 LORENZO BOTURINI BENADUCCI, 1702–1755
Idea De Una Nueva Historia General De La America Septentrional....
En Madrid: En la Imprenta de Juan de Zuñiga. Año M.D.CC.XLVI [1746].

Boturini, a Milanese nobleman, went to Mexico in 1735 in order to trace the historical origins of the veneration of Our Lady of Guadalupe. Between the years 1736 and 1743 he traveled and lived among the Indians least tainted by European culture and studied their ways. During those seven years he assembled a collection of Mexican-Indian manuscripts that, according to Dr. John B. Glass, who has studied Boturini, "was the most important collection for Mexican ethno-history ever assembled." Boturini's research led him into study of Aztec culture and religion, and he became engrossed in the subject. While Church officials considered it defunct and knew little about it, Boturini found that the religion was still alive in many remote areas. His study of native religion was potentially dangerous, and in 1743 he encountered difficulties with the Inquisition. He was arrested, his collection confiscated, and he was deported to Spain. Deprived of his manuscripts, he still published this book on the conquest of Mexico. The first part deals with Indian codices and how to read them. It also contains much material on native religion. The latter portion of the book is a catalogue of his manuscript collection. Boturini's collection was dispersed, but the concept behind it, his idea of a new kind of history, was fundamental to historians and anthropologists of succeeding generations.

JCB(1)3:817; José Toribio Medina, *Biblioteca hispanoamericana, 1493–1810*, Santiago de Chile, 1898–1907, 3408; Sabin 6834.
Acquired before 1859 by John Carter Brown.

66 RAIMONDO DI SANGRO, PRINCIPE DE SANSEVERO, 1710–1771
Lettera Apologetica Dell'Esercitato Accademico Della Crusca Contenente La Difesa del Libro Intitolato Lettere D'Una Peruana Per rispetto alla supposizione De' Quipu Scritta Alla Duchessa Di S****....
In Napoli MDCCL [1750].

Raimondo di Sangro was born at Torremaggiore (Foggia) of one of the most powerful noble families of the kingdom of Naples. He was educated by Jesuits and learned numerous languages. After military service as a young man, he devoted his life to mechanical invention, study, and writing. The striking title page of this book—printed in orange, green, and black—was produced by a process invented by him. The *Enciclo-*

pedia Italiana says of him: "His bizarre and acute genius, helped by a little charlatanry, yielded him a reputation throughout Italy and beyond."

In this book the Prince defends *Lettres d'une Peruvienne*, published anonymously by Madame Graffigny, Paris, 1747. Her novel consists of thirty-eight letters supposedly written by the Inca Princess Zilia to her lover Aza. The letters were written in *Quipu* of the Incas according to Graffigny. *Quipu* are cords, usually about two feet in length, composed of varicolored threads. The word *quipu* itself means knot, and, by a system of color-coding the threads and making patterns with the knots, the Incas recorded statistical information. The Prince believed that *Quipu* was a writing system and defended Madame Graffigny from detractors of her fiction. In defending the veracity of a fiction, di Sangro was off the mark, yet his book is the earliest full study of the *Quipu* writing system.

JCB (1)3:932; Sabin 40560.
Acquired before 1870 by John Carter Brown.

XII *Italian Influence on the Arts in Colonial America*

THE place of Italy in the history of opera, music, and architecture requires no comment, but what is not as well known is how and when the tradition of Italian art began to be imported into the New World. Three items, all known only in the copies in this exhibition (as far as we can determine), represent Italian contributions in three arts. One book was printed at Lima, one at Mexico City, one at Boston: they stand at the beginning at the vast impact Italian art has had in all of America.

67 SILVIO STAMPIGLIA, 1664–1725
La Partenope Fiesta, que se hizo en el Real Palacio de Mexico....
En México por los Herederos de la Viuda de Miguel de Ribera [ca. 1760].

The first opera of any sort produced on American soil. The opera was first performed in Naples in 1699. It was staged in Spanish translation in Mexico City in 1711, and the text—both the original Italian and the translation on facing pages—was printed there some decades later.

Acquired 1907. Endowment funds.

68 FRANCESCO GEMINIANI, 1680–1762
An Abstract Of Geminiani's Art Of Playing Violin....
Boston, New-England: Printed by John Boyles, 1769.

Geminiani was a notable composer and a violin teacher in London where this beginner's handbook was first published in 1740. The publication of such a manual indicates that society in the English colonies had become sophisticated enough to allow an audience for secular music. The first professional musicians appear at about this time, as do the first American composers. This is the only known copy of the first music book of its kind printed in the United States.

JCBAR 31:16–18; Roger P. Bristol, *Supplement to Charles Evans' American Bibliography*, Charlottesville, Virginia, 1970, 3000; *Colonial Scene*, pp. 104–105.
Acquired 1931. Endowment funds.

69 MIGUEL SUÁREZ DE FIGUEROA
Templo De N. Grande Patriarca San Francisco De La Provincia De los doze Apostoles de el Peru....
En Lima, Año de 1675.

The attempts of Italian humanistic architects to incorporate Neo-Platonic philosophy with Christian religion in building brought about a style that emphasized symmetry and light. The wave of Spanish friars who set out for Mexico in the 1520's had acquired the humanistic ideas which spread from Italy. They supervised the construction of humanistic Italian-style churches throughout Spanish America. There was a moral, as well as aesthetic, consideration to this architecture. Christian public architecture—as in cathedrals—was designed to contain spiritually and physically the entire population of the area it served. In contrast, the Aztec temples (see number 71) were reserved for the priests and their victims.

One of the great monuments of humanistic architecture in America is the cathedral of San Francisco in Lima. Our copy of the book describing the dedication of this cathedral in 1675 contains the only known engraving showing the entire church.

Medina, *Lima*, 496; Humberto Rodríguez Camilloni, "Architectural principles of the Age of Humanism applied," *Journal of the Society of Architectural Historians*, XXVIII, Dec. 1969, pp. 235–253; Humberto Rodríguez Camilloni, "El Conjuncto monumental de San Francisco De Lima en los siglos XVII y XVIII," in *Boletín Del Cento De Investigaciones Históricas y Estéticas*, XIV, Caracas, Venezuela, 1972, pp. 31–60.
Acquired 1968. Louisa Dexter Sharpe Metcalf Fund.

XIII *Jesuits from America Exiled to Italy*

IN 1608 the Jesuits were granted permission to organize the Guarani Indians of Paraguay. By the mid-eighteenth century, under their direction, a self-contained agricultural society flourished. In the 1740's, settlers from Spanish Argentina and Portuguese Brazil sought to acquire the productive Jesuit/Indian lands. Raids were staged. The Jesuits armed the natives and trained them to defend themselves. Battles ensued. Spain and Portugal came to terms, ignoring the Jesuits and Indians, splitting the lands between themselves in the Treaty of Madrid, 13 January 1750.

The Jesuits, outraged at the injustice, resisted implementation of the Treaty. Spain sent troops who removed the missionaries from Paraguay and, in the decade that followed, Spain and Portugal (and later France) expelled all Jesuits from their domains.

The Jesuits came from various countries, many were Italian, but there were few countries to which they could go freely in their exile. Many of them took refuge in the Papal States of Italy where in exile they wrote works which have become basic studies of much of South America.

70 JOSEPH JOLIS

Saggio Sulla Storia Naturale Della Provincia Del Gran Chaco. . . .
In Faenza MDCCLXXXIX [1789]. Por Lodovico Genestri.

A Catalan, Jolis had served in Paraguay for ten years when he was forceably removed. In 1767 he settled in Faenza in the Papal States. He planned a four-volume study of the Gran Chaco—the great lowland plain now shared by Paraguay, Argentina, and Bolivia—from which his order had been removed. He published only the first volume, rich in detailed anthropological information about native life and customs.

JCB(1)3:3288; Sabin 36411; Backer 4:812; Streit 3:1118.
Acquired before 1870 by John Carter Brown.

71 FRANCISCO JAVIER CLAVIJERO, 1731–1787

Storia Antica Del Messico Cavata Da' Migliori Storici Spagnuoli E Da' Manoscritti. . . .
In Cesena MDCCLXXX [1780]. Per Gregorio Biasini.

Clavijero was a native of Veracruz, Mexico, who taught rhetoric and philosophy at the University of Mexico before being exiled. In his enforced idleness, in the small city of Cesena in Romagna, he studied the early history of his country. His four-volume study of pre-conquest Mexico developed themes laid down by Boturini Benaducci (see number 65) and was an important step in the scientific study of Aztec civilization. The illustrations depicted an Aztec temple, studied from ruins, and dress and religious rites, derived from manuscript records.

JCB(1)3:2629; Sabin 13518; Backer 2:1210; Gerbi, *Dispute*, pp. 196–211.
Acquired before 1870 by John Carter Brown.

72 FILIPPO SALVATORE GILII, 1721–1789

Saggio Di Storia Americana. . . .
Roma, MDCCLXXX [1780]. Per Luigi Perego. . . .

A native of Spoleto, Gilii had spent eighteen years in a mission to the Orinoco region before being forced home. The four volumes he wrote during his exile are basic for the history of Venezuela. The first volume deals with geography and natural history, the second with native customs, the third with religion and language, and the fourth with the current situation in the area. King Charles III of Spain awarded Gilii a pension for his work. The illustrations for the book are an important record of native life on the South American frontier. The artist's classical training gives the figures an appearance more likely to be encountered in the Roman Forum than the jungles of the Orinoco, but the information conveyed is accurate.

JCB(1)3:2648; Sabin 7382; Backer 3:1415–16; Gerbi, *Dispute*, pp. 223–233.
Acquired before 1870 by John Carter Brown.

XIV *Italian Awareness of English America, 1750–1775*

THE growth of the English colonies in North America seems to have gone unnoticed throughout most of Europe. In 1755, just before the outbreak of the Seven Years' War, it has been said that in France all but a few individuals were "almost completely ignorant of conditions there." The same was true in Italy: we know of few Italian books printed before 1750 that even mention the settlements which were to become the United States. The outbreak of a war for empire between England and France over which nation would control North America—the Seven Years' War, 1756–1763—made Europeans aware of how powerful a resource the English colonies had become.

73 [JACQUES NICOLAS BELLIN] 1703–1772
Descrizione Geografica Di Parte Dell' America Settentrionale. . . .
Amsterdam, MDCCLVIII [1758]. E si vende in Venezia da Pietro Bassaglia Libraio. . . .

In this pamphlet and its map the stakes of the rivals for empire in North America are laid out. We believe it to be the work of the French cartographer Bellin who wrote a series of pamphlets in French with similar titles. Although we know of no other copy of this pamphlet, nor of a French original for this one, it fits Bellin's pattern of publication. It was not unusual at this time for works in Italian to be printed at Amsterdam and sold by booksellers in Venice.

Acquired 1911. Endowment funds.

74 MARC'ANTONIO BADIA
Compendio Della Guerra Nata Per Confini in America Tra La Francia, E L'Inghilterra. . . .
In Amsterdam [i.e., Venice?], 1763.

The Seven Years' War or, as it was known in America, the French and Indian War, changed the balance of power in Europe. Badia asks who could have imagined that France and England would fight such a ferocious war throughout the world simply over America? And who could have imagined that Britain and Prussia alone could so decisively defeat the combined powers of France, the German Emperor, Austria, Sweden, Russia, Saxony, and Spain? The growth of America had unbalanced the centuries-old power structure of Europe, and even more changes were to follow. Italian readers must have been deeply concerned about how this affected them.

This work appears to be Venetian printing: the Amsterdam imprint is probably false and is presumably a cover to protect the actual printer. As the losers in this war were powers that dominated Italian politics, frank discussion of the war would have been a delicate matter.

Sabin 2709.
Acquired before 1900.

75 ANONYMOUS
La Storia Dell'Anno MDCCLXIX [1769]. . . .
In Venezia. A spese di Francesco Pitteri [1770].

Italians obtained some American news from newspapers and from publications such as this annual survey of the events of the preceding year. The Library has fifteen of these from different years, the first printed in 1741, the last in 1796. In this issue the commercial disadvantages placed on Americans are explained as part of the reason for colonial unrest in 1769.

Acquired 1975. The gift of Mrs. Roger Amore Laudati.

76 ANTONIO GENOVESI, 1712-1769
Lezioni Di Commercio O Sia D'Economia Civile Dell'Ab. Antonio Genovesi. . . .
Bassano, MDCCLXIX [1769]. A Spese Remondini Di Venezia.

Antonio Genovesi was Professor of Economics at the University of Naples, the first professorship in that field ever established. He trained a generation of students who served King Charles III in Naples, Spain, and the New World. Genovesi's book, first published at Naples in 1766, is filled with American examples which display a deep familiarity with the literature on America. Perhaps most interesting is his projection that, at the current rate of growth, the wealth of England's and Spain's American colonies would outstrip that of the metropolitan countries. Then, he suggests, as it is unnatural for the greater to be dominated by the lesser, surely the Americas will have to become independent.

Pace, *Franklin*, p. 125; Kenneth E. Carpenter, *Economic Bestsellers before 1850*, Cambridge, Massachusetts, 1975.
Acquired 1975. Associates of the John Carter Brown Library.

77 [GOTTFRIED ACHENWALL] 1719-1772
Précis De L'État Actuel Des Colonies Angloises Dans l'Amérique Septentrionale. . . .
A Milan. MDCCLXXI [1771]. Chez Les Frères Reycends. . . .

This book is a plagiarism, published by Dominique Blackford, of the *Anmerkungen* (the notes) of Gottfried Achenwall, a professor at Göttingen University. Achenwall had interviewed Benjamin Franklin during the latter's visit to the Göttingen in 1766. The results of the interview, the *Anmerkungen*, were published in the *Hannoverisches Magazin* in three installments in 1767 and then published separately in 1769.

Blackford presented the translated text as his own, and it was widely reviewed in Italian magazines. The book included a copy of Benjamin Franklin's testimony on the Stamp Act in America before the English House of Commons in 1766, and introduced the arguments of the American patriots to Italy. While the libertarian pamphlets published by Americans were well received in certain circles, few were translated into Italian or printed in Italy. Most Italian intellectuals knew them from French translations, if not from the original English.

Leonard N. Beck, "Dominique de Blackford: Plagiarist," *Bibliographical Society of America, Papers*, vol. 68 (1974), pp. 427-432; Pace, *Franklin*, p. 124; Sabin 5691.
Acquired 1946. Associates of the John Carter Brown Library.

78 VINCENZO MARTINELLI
Istoria Del Governo D'Inghilterra E Delle Sue Colonie In India,
E Nell'America Settentrionale. . . .
   In Firenze MDCCLXXVI [1776]. Per Gaetano Cambiagi. . . .

This book was one of the first histories of the American Revolution. Martinelli, a prominent Florentine writer who had known Benjamin Franklin in London, appreciated the Americans' patriotic motivation. He combined such notions as Pennsylvania being the realization of a poetic Golden Age with more realistic assessments of America's resources. In his judgment England was involved in a war in which they could suffer shameful losses and could gain only lamentable victories. The book was reprinted at Pescia, near Lucca, in 1777.

Pace, *Franklin,* pp. 168, 238–239. Sabin 44946 is the Pescia edition.
Acquired before 1900.

79 GUILLAUME THOMAS FRANÇOIS RAYNAL, 1713–1796
Storia Dell'America Settentrionale. . . .
   Venezia, Dalle Stampe Di Antonio Zatta. . . . M.DCC.LXXVIII [1778]. Three volumes.

The most widely-read author on America during the years after 1770 was the Abbé Raynal. He never traveled to America, but he believed that the discovery of America had been "both the most important and most disastrous event in the history of civilization." In this spirit, he compiled an encyclopaedic work, *Histoire Philosophique et Politique* . . . , which first appeared in Amsterdam, 1770. With revisions and additions, the work went through many editions in French and was translated into various European languages. The book was controversial on many grounds. His strong opposition to colonies aroused leaders of colonial powers against him. His theory that the climate of America caused plants, animals, and people to deteriorate into inferior forms inspired replies by many Americans from Jefferson of Virginia to José Hipólito Unanue of Lima.

   The Venice edition is an Italian translation of the seventeenth and eighteenth books of Raynal's second version of the text first published at The Hague in 1774. This is the portion of the book that dealt with British North America. Most of Raynal's book dealt with Spanish America, and the sources of his theories were Spanish. Antonio Zatta chose to publish that part of the book which had topical interest. Zatta published a number of geographical works, including an atlas with a special section of North American maps, and other Americana during the succeeding twenty-five years.

Acquired 1972. Associates of the John Carter Brown Library.

80 [WILLIAM KNOX] 1732–1810
Stato Presente Della Nazione Inglese Sopratutto concernente il suo Commercio
e le sue finanze. . . .
   In Napoli MDCCLXXV [1775], Per Vincenzo Flauto. . . .

William Knox had been Governor of Georgia, an agent in London for several colonies and Under-Secretary of State for America during the years 1770 to 1782. He knew the American situation intimately, and as relations between England and her colonies deteriorated during the Stamp Act crisis he wrote a gloomy appraisal of Britain's financial situation, *The Present State of the Nation*, first published in London, 1768. His forty-eight-page pamphlet went through four editions in London and one in Dublin and generated controversy: it was attacked by Edmund Burke among other English writers.

Knox's pamphlet had unusually wide circulation abroad: the John Carter Brown Library has three Spanish editions (of 1770, 1771, and 1781) and a French edition of 1769. As this catalogue was in the final stages of preparation the Neapolitan edition of a translation became available. The translator, Michele Torchia, added to Knox's modest work, expanding it into two volumes of over 350 pages, and dedicated it to Marchese Bernardo Tanucci, the Tuscan Regent of Naples. In Torchia's hands the book became a plea for free trade in the kingdom. Torchia was well versed in the English system and the important role the American colonies played in the system. His additions include more American material: the second volume includes the memorial from the Continental Congress of 5 September 1774 to the people of Britain in which the plight of the colonists is presented directly to the populace.

Kress Library of Business and Economics, Harvard University, *Catalogue*, Boston, 1940, 7126.
Acquired 1979. The gift of Mr. and Mrs. Samuel J. Hough to honor Mr. and Mrs. Vincent J. Buonanno.

81 ANONYMOUS
Il Gazzettiere Americano Contenente Un Distinto Ragguaglio Di Tutte Le Parti Del Nuovo Mondo....
In Livorno Per Marco Coltellini ... MDCCLXIII [1763].

This is a translation of an anonymous English book, *The American Gazetteer*, published in London by Andrew Miller the previous year. The translator is not known, but he faithfully rendered the English into Italian. A comparison of the entries shows that although the words were translated literally the printer, Marco Coltellini, has elevated the cramped, unattractive English original into a handsome book, and the visual effect of the Italian edition is strikingly superior. Because it is a translation of an English work, there is much more information about the English colonies in America than is found in most geographical books written by continental authors up to this time.

JCB(1)3:1355; Sabin 26814.
Acquired before 1870 by John Carter Brown.

XV *Benjamin Franklin and the Italians*

FOR many Italians in the second half of the eighteenth century, Benjamin Franklin represented Anglo-America. They became aware of him in 1752, as a result of his electrical experiments, at the same time as they were becoming aware of the potential of English North America. For the next forty years Franklin's writings and character made deep impressions on Italians.

82 GIUSEPPE ANTONIO FRANCESCO GIROLAMO EANDI, 1735–1799

Memorie Istoriche Intorno Gli Studi Del Padre Giambatista Beccaria. Delle Scuole Pie. . . .

MDCCLXXXIII [1783]. Colophon: Dalla Stamperia Reale Di Torino.

Franklin's connection with Italian scientists is represented by this biographical notice of Father Giambatista Beccaria, professor at the University of Turin. Beccaria had responded to Franklin's electrical experiments by conducting a series of important experiments himself. Letters exchanged between Franklin and the learned Beccaria are appended to this work.

Pace, *Franklin*, p. 418, n. 50.
Acquired 1974. Louisa Dexter Sharpe Metcalf Fund.

83 BENJAMIN FRANKLIN, 1706–1790

Scelta Di Lettere E Di Opuscoli Del Signor Beniamino Franklin Tradotti Dall'Inglese.

In Milano, MDCCLXXIV [1774]. Nella Stampería di Giuseppe Marelli.

This first selection of Franklin's scientific works to appear in Italian was taken from the French *Oeuvres*, published in Paris, 1773, by Barbeau Dubourg. The Italian translator, Carlo Giuseppe Campi, dedicated the collection to Count Carlo Giuseppe Firmian, the Governor of Lombardy, explaining that his motive was to make "better known to the world the name, the merit, and the teachings of this great philosopher."

Ford (*Franklin*) 321; Pace, *Franklin*, p. 45, n. 12.
Acquired 1920. Endowment fund.

84 BENJAMIN FRANKLIN, 1706–1790

Opere Politiche. . . .

In Padova, MDCCLXXXIII [1783].

This collection was translated by the Venetian abbot Pietro Antoniutti from Benjamin Vaughan's edition of Franklin's *Political, Miscellaneous, and Philosophical Pieces*, London, 1779. It marks a turn of Italian interest in Franklin: there was more interest in his political writings than in his earlier scientific works as a result of increased awareness of the significance of the American war.

Ford (*Franklin*) 343; Pace, *Franklin*, p. 128.
Acquired 1968. Associates of the John Carter Brown Library.

85 BENJAMIN FRANKLIN, 1706–1790

Descrizione Della Stufa Di Pensilvania. . . .

In Venezia, MDCCLXXXVIII [1788]. Nella Stamperia Graziosi a S. Apollinare.

Italians were very interested in Franklin's stove. In 1767 Leopold, Grand Duke of Tuscany, sent Filippo Mazzei to London to purchase one. Franklin himself helped Mazzei obtain a correctly made version, and

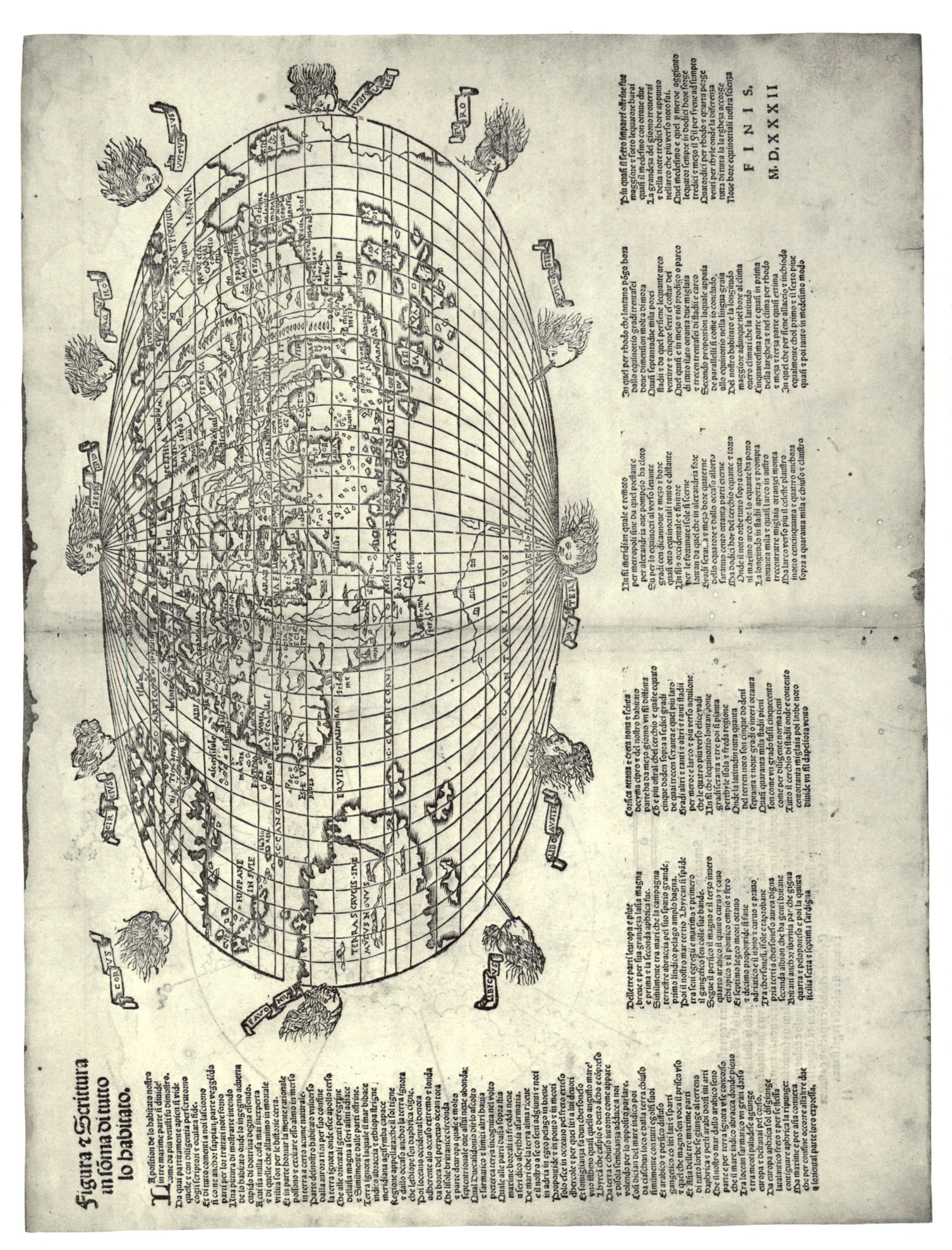

XIV (cat. no. 98) Bartolommeo da li Sonetti. World Map. Venice, 1532. [Map of ca. 1520.] 40 × 20 cm. *Courtesy of the Joseph S. Sinclair Family Trust.*

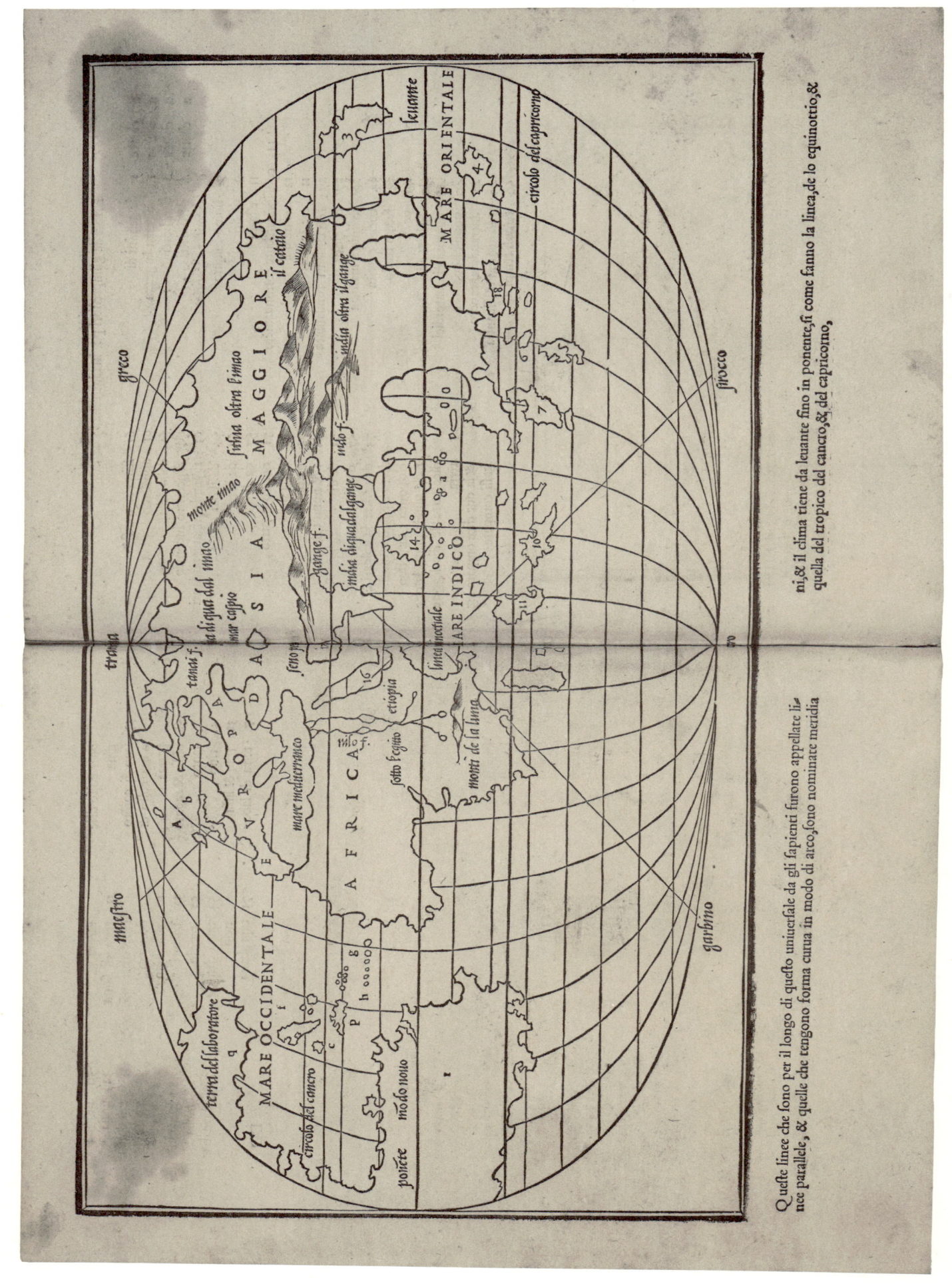

XV (cat. no. 99) Bordone. World Map. Venice, 1532. 43×20 cm.

XVI (cat. no. 102) Vavassore. World Map. [Venice, 1525?] 43 × 57 cm.

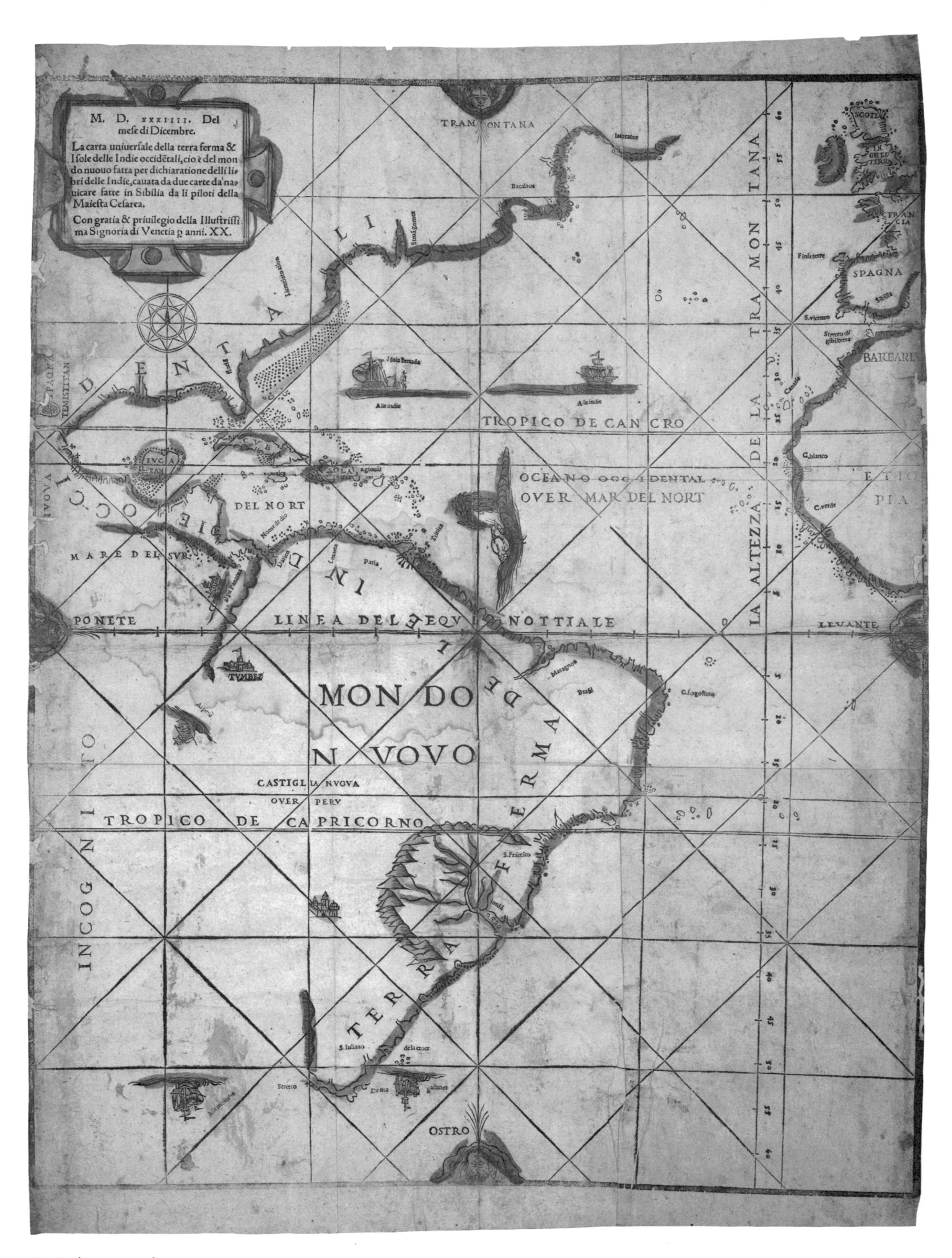

XVII (cat. no. 103)   Ramusio. *Carta Universale*. Venice, 1534. 56×57 cm. *Courtesy of Mr. and Mrs. George Conley.*

XVIII (cat. no. 106) "Florentine Goldsmith's Map." [Florence? 1544?] 29×21 cm.

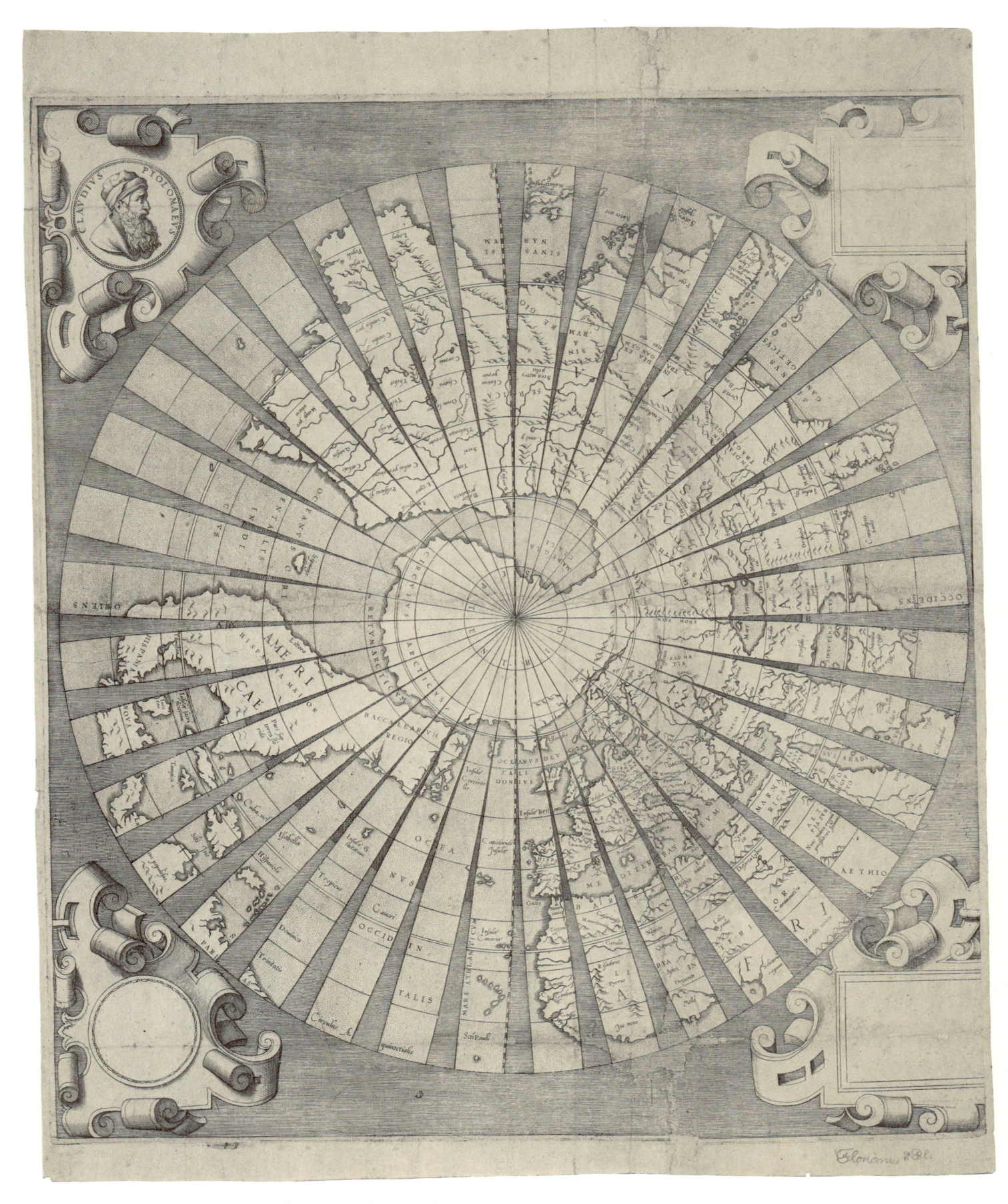

XIX (cat. no. 114)   Florian. Northern Hemisphere. Venice, 1556. 43×47.5 cm.

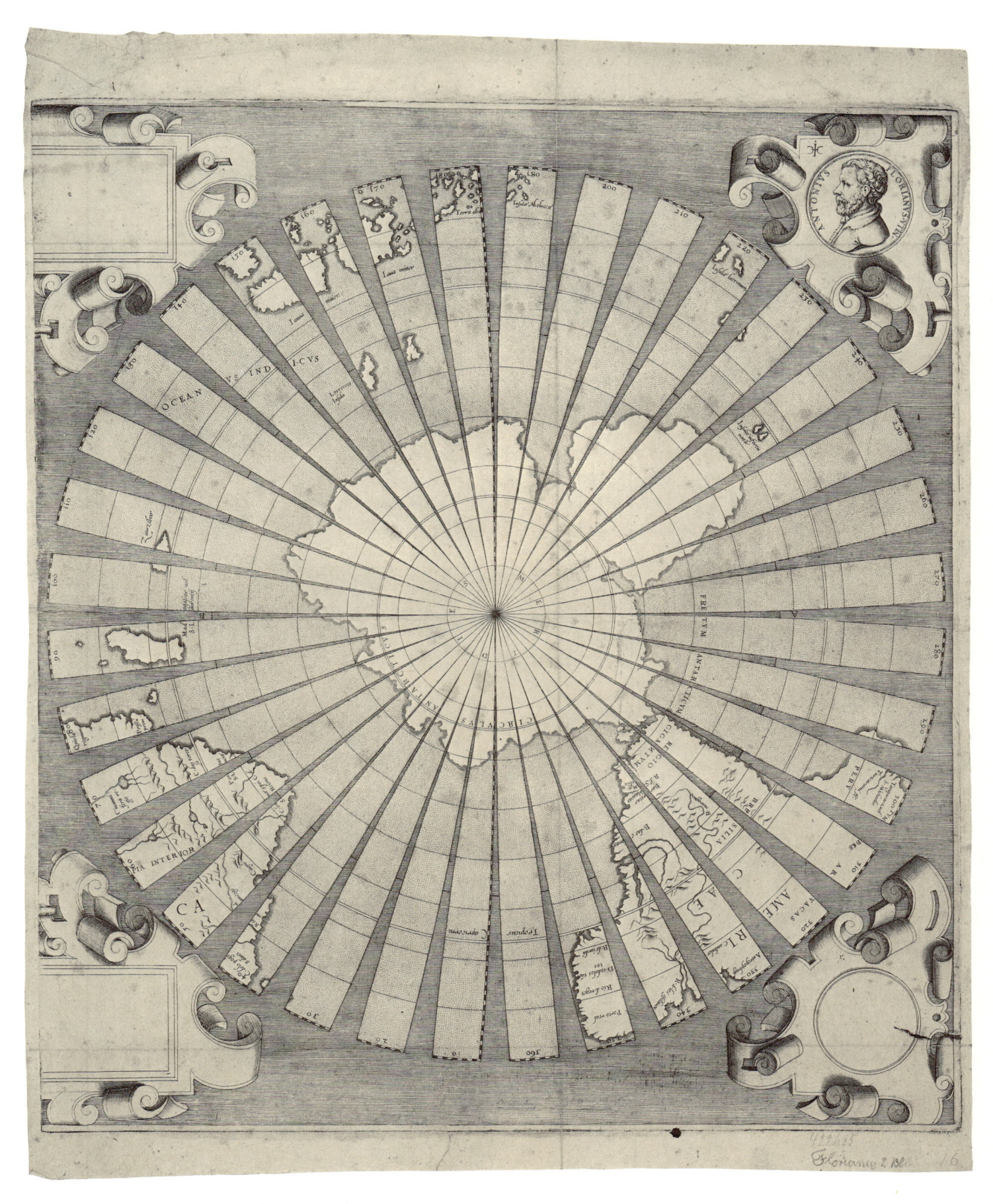

XX (cat. no. 114)   Florian. Southern Hemisphere. Venice, 1556. 43×47.5 cm.

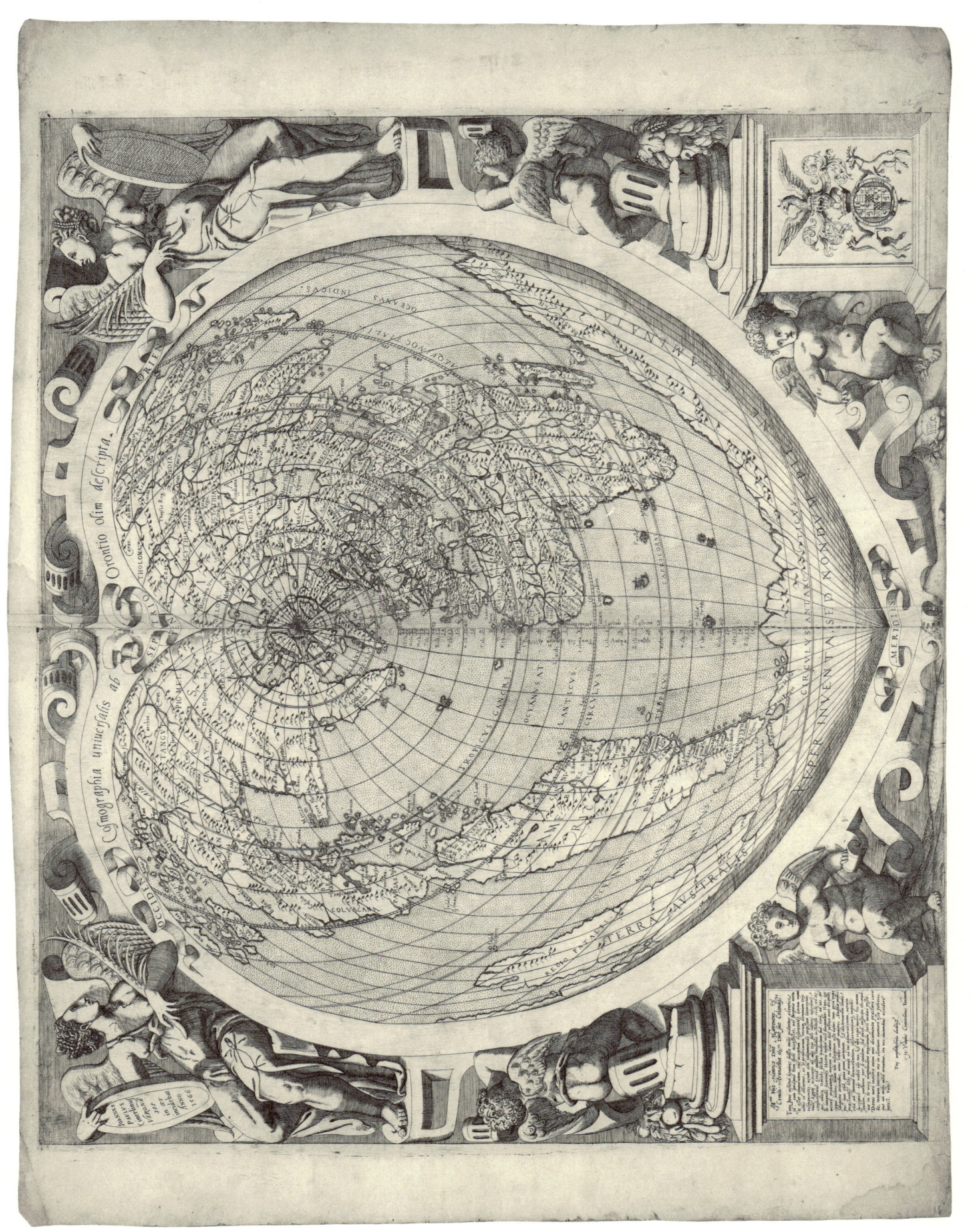

XXI (cat. no. 119) Fine. Cordiform World Map. [Venice, 1566.] 59 × 51.5 cm.

as a consequence the first authentic Franklin stove in Europe was to be found in Florence. Word of its effectiveness spread, and soon the stoves were available in Milan, Venice, and other cities. The Venetian printer Antonio Graziosi first published this pamphlet in 1778 and brought out editions of 1781, 1788, and 1791 (of which the Library has the last two), besides advertising it annually in his newspaper, *Notizie del Mondo*.

Pace, *Franklin*, p. 76, cf. p. 417, n. 35; cf. Ford (*Franklin*) 42.
Acquired 1958. Associates of the John Carter Brown Library.

86 [BENJAMIN FRANKLIN] 1706–1790
Avviso A Quegli Che Pensassero D'Andare In America....
In Cremona, Per Lorenzo Manini Regio Stampatore. 1785.

This is a translation of Franklin's *Two Tracts*, London, 1784, which included "Information to Those who Would remove to America" and "Remarks concerning the Savages of North America." Franklin composed the first tract to discourage "misfits" from coming to America, including artists, office-seekers, soldiers, and nobility. America was for those who were willing to work. The second tract pictured Indians as simple, virtuous people of common sense. Two different Italian translations were published in 1785, this one by the Cremonese printer Lorenzo Manini.

Pace, *Franklin*, p. 140.
Acquired 1972. Lathrop Colgate Harper Fund.

87 [BENJAMIN FRANKLIN] 1706–1790
Il Buon Uomo Ricciardo E La Costituzione Di Pensilvania Italianizzati Per Uso Delle Democratica Veneta Ristaurazione.
Venezia, 1797.

The European political struggles of the 1790's put tremendous pressure on all the Italian states and caused the structure of the Venetian oligarchy to collapse. For a brief time a democratic government was proclaimed, but in 1797 the French and, later, the Austrians installed their own oppressive rule over the city. In the brief period when democratic aspirations flamed, two young patriots published this book. It translates the aphorisms Franklin had published in his almanacs and the Constitution of Pennsylvania (which Franklin had helped to write) for the use of the restoration of Venetian democracy. The political examples of Franklin and of Pennsylvania offered a promise the Venetians were unable to realize for three generations.

There is no copy of this book known to be in another American library, and only two have been identified in European collections.

Plate XII.

Pace, *Franklin*, p. 421, n. 87.
Acquired 1977. Anonymous gift to honor Senator John H. Pastore.

XVI *Italian Contributions to American Political Thought*

THE founders of the American republic owed much to Italians. At one level there were the writers on political and social problems. Then there were the examples of the Italian republics which survived into the eighteenth century—Venice, Genoa, San Marino, and Lucca. Finally, in the 1760's there was the stirring struggle of Pasquale Paoli's Corsicans to free their island from foreign domination. Paoli, Pennsylvania, not far from Valley Forge, was named by its settlers for a patriot they were soon to emulate.

88 CESARE BONESANA MARCHESE DI BECCARIA, 1738–1794
An Essay On Crimes And Punishments. . . .
Philadelphia: Printed and Sold by R. Bell . . . M.DCC.LXXVIII [1778].

One of the profoundly revolutionary works of a revolutionary era was Beccaria's essay on the relationship of the individual to the state. Beccaria developed the idea of the difference between sin and crime, stating that the former is God's concern, and proposing humane civil resolution of the latter. First published at Leghorn in 1764, his *Dei delitti e delle pene* was translated into French by Abbé Andre Morellet in 1766 and, with notes by Voltaire, the French was translated into English. Four editions of the English translation were printed in the United States (in 1773, 1777, 1778, and 1793). Beccaria's humane approach to incarceration was incorporated into the first United States penitentiary, which was built in Philadelphia in 1791.

Evans 15730; Franco Venturi, *Utopia and Reform in the Enlightenment*, Cambridge U.P., 1971, pp. 100–116.
Acquired 1914. Endowment funds.

89 BENJAMIN FRANKLIN, 1706–1790
Rules For Reducing A Great Empire To A Small One. . . .
London: Printed for James Ridgway . . . 1793.

Franklin's political "rules" are modeled upon Machiavelli's *Prince*. They were first printed in 1772 in *The Public Advertiser*, a London newspaper, and this is their first separate publication. The shrewd advice, given tongue in cheek, was intended to point out to British politicians the way to wiser handling of America, as Machiavelli had intended to point out the folly of tyrannical rule.

JCB(1)3:3593; Sabin 25580; Ford (*Franklin*) 314.
Acquired 1871 by John Carter Brown.

90 JOHN ADAMS, 1735–1826
A Defence Of The Constitutions of Government Of The United States Of America. . . .
Philadelphia: Printed for Hall and Sellers. . . . M.DCC.LXXXVII [1787].

In 1787, the confederation of states that made up the United States lacked central direction. John Adams, soon to be Washington's Vice-President and later President, wrote of the changes that were required to develop a balanced constitution. Adams believed that society was divided into two basically antagonistic classes, the wealthy and the poor, and that the constitution should not allow either group to dominate the state. He explored the experience of Italian republics in resolving class problems. In the first section of this book, entitled "Democratical Republics," his first example is San Marino; the second section, "Aristocratical Republics," includes Genoa, Lucca, and Venice as examples of systems from which Americans could learn. Machiavelli's *Discourses* are also cited in Adams's discussion of mixed governments.

Evans 20177. Gordon S. Wood, "The Relevance and Irrelevance of John Adams," in *The Creation of the American Republic, 1776–1787*, Chapel Hill, 1969, pp. 567–592.
Acquired 1914. Endowment funds.

XVII *Italians and the American Revolution*

THE American war was at first perceived by Frenchmen, Italians, and other Europeans as the overthrow of British political and economic domination. To this theme Italians were particularly sympathetic, and the example of the thirteen American colonies—each with its own interests, each maintaining a degree of sovereign power but working together to accomplish common goals—had special meaning. As the war continued and Italians learned more about it, perceptions of its significance changed. The struggle was also seen as a revolt of an entire people against the tyranny of absolute power, a mass assertion of the inalienable rights of man. This social aspect of the Revolution was greeted with enthusiasm or regretted, according to the individual's political vantage.

91 VITTORIO ALFIERI, 1749–1803
L'America Libera Odi Di Vittorio Alfieri Da Asti. . . .
Dalla Tipografia Di Kehl . . . M.DCC.LXXXIV [1784].

L'America Libera consists of five odes on the American Revolution. The first four odes were written in 1781 and deal with the causes of the war; the fourth ode is on General Washington and begins: *Tu, rapitor del fulmine celeste.* The fifth ode, written in 1783, is on the Peace of that year. Pierre A. C. Beaumarchais, wealthy trader, playwright, secret political agent in the American cause, had the odes printed at the private press on his estate at Kehl across from Strasbourg on the Rhine.

Plate XIII.

The modern edition is found in *Rime di Vittorio Alfieri secondo le edizioni originale e gli autografi*, ed. Francesco Maggini, Florence, 1933, pp. 282–311.
Acquired 1949. Associates of the John Carter Brown Library.

92 [VITTORIO ALFIERI] 1749–1803
La Guerra in America.
[Italy? or Paris? ca. 1784. Manuscript.]

This manuscript version of Alfieri's *L'America Libera* may have been prepared for sending to America. We know that Alfieri sent manuscript copies of his odes to Washington and to other American leaders, and this may be one of those manuscripts. Alfieri changed his text several times before it was printed for the first time at Kehl; the text in this manuscript is one of the intermediary versions before the printing.

Franco Fido, "A proposito di un manoscritto dell'America libera'," *Giornale Storico della Letteratura Italiana*, 149 (1972), pp. 469–475; Ernest Hatch Wilkins, "Alfieri in America," in *The Invention of the Sonnet and Other Studies in Italian Literature*, Rome, 1959, pp. 295–313.
Acquired 1966. The gift of Mrs. Roger Amore Laudati.

93 VITTORIO ALFIERI, 1749–1803
L'America Libera Odi.
Italia, MDCCCV [1805].

This is the only early edition of Alfieri's *Odi* to be printed in Italy. "Italia" was a geographical concept which had never been realized as a political entity and therefore the use of the imprint "Italia" was an act of political defiance against the French and Austrians who ruled the peninsula. The pertinence of the American struggle to cast out foreign rulers to the aspirations of Italian patriots is made in this simple but bold stroke.

Gamba 2529.
Acquired 1969. Associates of the John Carter Brown Library.

94 GIOVANNI RINALDO CARLI, 1720–1795
Delle Lettere Americane. . . .
Cosmopoli [i.e., Florence], MDCCLXXX [1780].

The learned Count Carli combined extensive readings in history, literature, science, economics, and philosophy in this book. The *Lettere* were written to refute the commonly circulated idea among some European thinkers that America supported inferior life forms. Carli wrote that the spirit of America created in liberty and toleration would provide an example for Europeans to follow. The letters in this book, written in 1777–1778 and first published in the *Magazzino Toscano* in 1780, were reprinted at Cremona in 1781–1783, and were published in French and German translations.

Sabin 10911; Pace, *Franklin*, pp. 135–139; Gerbi, *Dispute*, pp. 233–239.
Acquired 1920. Endowment funds.

95 FILIPPO MAZZEI, 1730–1816
Recherches Historiques Et Politiques Sur Les États-Unis De L'Amérique Septentrionale. . . .
A Colle, Et se trouve à Paris, Chez Froullé . . . 1788. Four volumes.

The Florentine Filippo Mazzei knew the United States more intimately and was more involved in American life and politics than any other Italian of the eighteenth century. He was a close friend of Thomas Jefferson and owned an estate, which he called Colle, near Jefferson's Monticello. He served as the agent of Virginia to the Grand Duke of Tuscany in 1776. He began writing his *Recherches* in 1785 to defend the United States from some of its critics. He believed that the new republic was an example of how political and intellectual freedom permitted a society to develop fully and progress. But Mazzei was not a propagandist: he was as concerned about inaccurate praise as about unwarranted criticisms. His *Recherches*, published in French in four volumes, was the fullest account the United States had available to Europeans at the time. The first volume is a historical-constitutional history of the United States; the second and third are rebuttals of two books critical of the country; and the fourth is a collection of essays on a variety of subjects.

Mazzei planned to have an Italian edition published at Florence, but nothing seems to have come of the project.

JCB (1)3:3208; Sabin 47206; E. Millicent Sowerby, *Catalogue of the Library of Thomas Jefferson*, Washington, Library of Congress, 3005; Gerbi, *Dispute*, pp. 268–275.
Acquired before 1870 by John Carter Brown.

96 LUIGI CASTIGLIONI, 1756–1832
Viaggio Negli Stati Uniti Dell' America Settentrionale fatto negli anni 1785, 1786, e 1787....
Milano, Nella Stamperia di Giuseppe Marelli ... 1790. Two volumes.

"The revolution that occurred in North America in recent years is one of the most momentous events of this century and could with time produce important consequences relating to Europe." With this opening passage, the Milanese count and botanist Luigi Castiglioni stated the importance he gave to the United States. Castiglioni arrived at Boston in May 1785 to examine for himself the political order that was forming, as well as to study American flora. Castiglioni traveled in all thirteen states and his descriptions are vivid, detailed, and mostly favorable. Even when shocked by the political disorder and monetary policy which he considered to be democratic excesses, he excused them as a phase through which the new nation had to pass.

JCB (1)3:3356; Sabin 11413; Antonio Pace, "The American Philosophical Society and Italy," in *Proceedings of the American Philosophical Society*, vol. 90, n. 5 (27 Dec. 1946), pp. 392–397.
Acquired before 1870 by John Carter Brown.

97 CARLO GIUSEPPE GUGLIELMO BOTTA, 1766–1837
Storia Della Guerra Dell' Independenza Degli Stati Uniti D' America.
Parigi, Per D. Colas, Stampatore, E Librajo ... Anno 1809.

This work grew out of a conversation held in 1806 in which those present were asked which modern event would make the most suitable theme for an heroic poem. All agreed that the American Revolution was the best subject. Botta interpreted the American cause as a struggle for liberty. At every opportunity he excited the nationalistic aspirations of the Italians, and suggested analogies with Italy's past and contemporary history. Botta looked upon the creation of the United States as an example and inspiration for the formation of an Italy unified and free of foreign rule.

Pace, *Franklin*, p. 170.
Acquired 1967. Louisa Dexter Sharpe Metcalf Fund.

XVIII *The Italian Cartographic Tradition*

THERE were three reasons for Italian superiority in cartography: a centuries-old tradition of portolan chartmaking; access to abundant and accurate information; and a skill in the art of engraving which advanced concurrently with the increase of information about America. *Portolani* were books of sailing directions, with charts of harbors, seacoasts, etc. They were designed solely for mariners and contained coastal details, but information about the interior is neglected or omitted entirely. By the time of the Age of Discovery, portolan maps had been made for several centuries, and their makers had achieved a conventional, geometrical style recognized by all.

The art of engraving was developed by goldsmiths, who first used the technique to record their ornate designs. In about 1450 some goldsmiths began making copperplate prints. During the next century Italian artists elevated copperplate engravings to very high levels. The technique was most appropriate for mapmaking as it allowed great detail to be recorded with clarity and precision.

The contributions which Italian mapmakers made toward the concept of the American continent and the dissemination of knowledge of America are so considerable as to deserve their own separate section.

THE ISOLARIOS

98 BARTOLOMMEO DA LI SONETTI
[Isolario.]
[Venice, 1532.]

By the time of the great explorers there was already in Italy a tradition of maritime mapmaking several centuries old. This book and the next two continue a *genre* begun in the 1420's when Cristoforo Buondelmonte, a Florentine, wrote a description of the Aegean Islands which, with many illustrating maps, was copied frequently. Buondelmonte's text survives in many manuscripts; it was not printed until this century. The fashion for books about islands, *isolarios*, continued after Buondelmonte. Three later authors imitated the form. The first printed *isolario* is that of Bartolommeo da li Sonetti published in Venice in 1485. When the book was reprinted in 1532 a world map was added to bring the work up to date. This map, by the Florentine Francesco Roselli (1445–1520), had been made much earlier in the century and is an important record of the Cabot voyage of 1497 as well as of Columbus's fourth voyage.

Plate XIV.

JCBAR 57:16, 20–22; *World Encompassed* 82; George E. Nunn, *World Map of Francisco Roselli*, Philadelphia, 1928.
Acquired 1957. The gift of George H. Beans.

99 BENEDETTO BORDONE, 1460–1530
Libro Di Benedetto Bordone Nel qual si ragiona da tutte l'Isole del mondo. . . .
Colophon: Impresse in Vinegia per Nicolo d'Aristotile . . . M.D.XXVIII [1528].

This is an *isolario* which goes beyond the traditional Mediterranean limits of earlier versions and includes the islands of Iceland, Ireland, England, the West Indies, eight Asian islands, and others. A view of Mexico

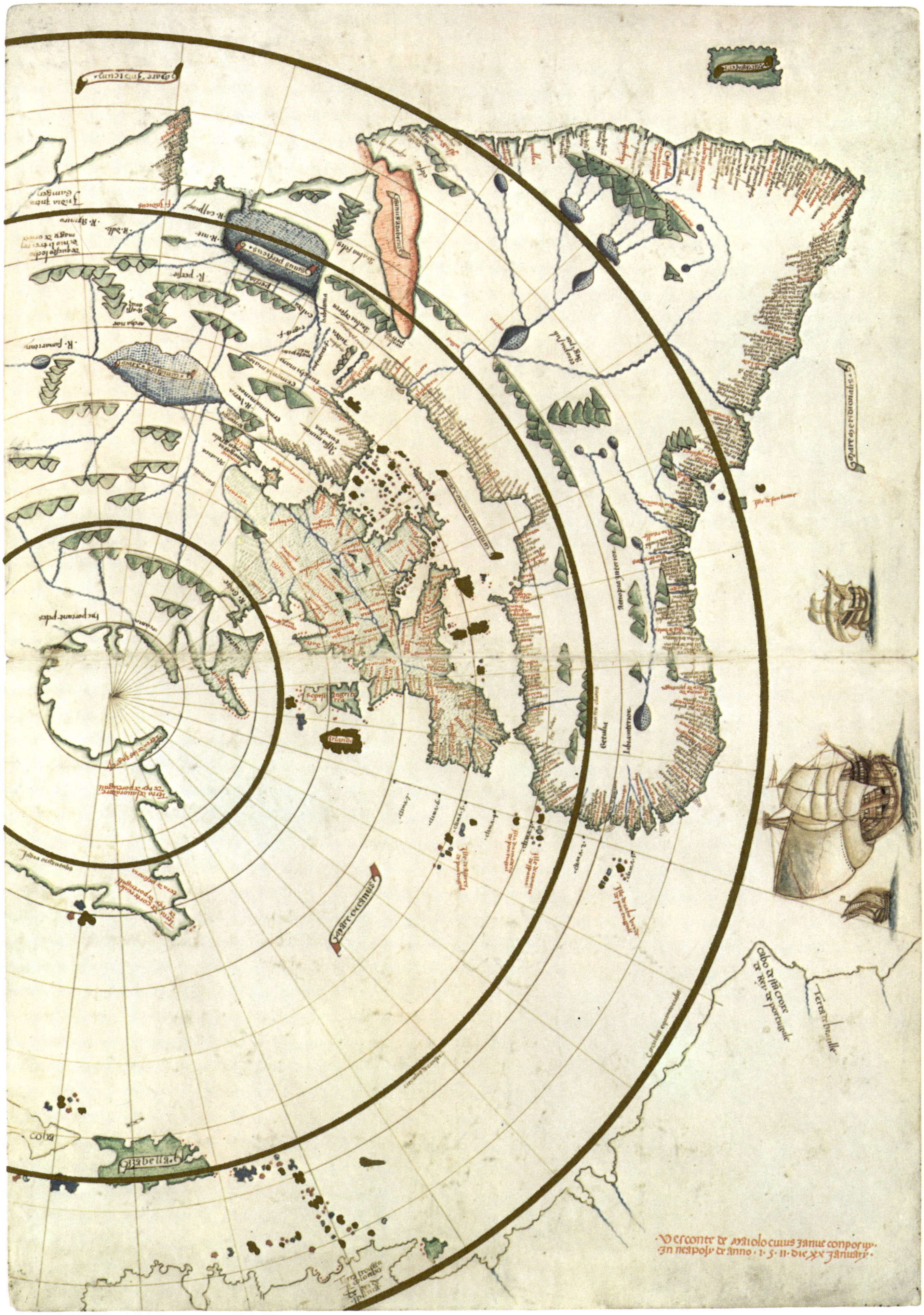

coba
Isabella
Irlanda
Mare oceanus
Vesconte de Maiolo civis Janue conposuy
In neapoly de anno 1 5 11 die XX January

I (cat. no. 101) Vesconte Maggiolo. World Map. Naples, 1511. 39×56 cm. *Courtesy of the Settipane family in memory of Joseph Settipane.*

City made by Cortés is included since it was located on an island. The book contains the first oval world map to have been printed although the Roselli map, not printed until 1532, had been drawn before this one.

Plate XV.

JCB(3)1:98–99; Sabin 6417; R. A. Skelton, "Introduction" to facsimile, Amsterdam, Theatrum Orbis Terrarum, 1966; *World Encompassed* 83; Myriam Billanovich, "Benedetto Bordon e Giulio Cesare Scaligero," in *Italia Medioevale e Umanistica*, XI (1968), pp. 187–256 (see esp. pp. 195–201).
Acquired before 1865 by John Carter Brown.

100   TOMASO PORCACCHI DA CASTIGLIONE, 1530–1585

L'Isole Piu Famose Del Mondo Descritte Da Thomaso Porcacchi Da Castiglione Arretino....
In Venetia. Appresso Simon Galignani & Girolamo Porro. MDLXXII [1572].

The series of *isolarios* reaches its culmination in this work by Porcacchi who was born about the time Bordone died. The engraved maps achieve detail, exactness, and an artistic richness of engraving not present in the earlier, simpler works.

JCB(3)1:250; Sabin 64148; *World Encompassed* 86.
Acquired 1846 by John Carter Brown.

101   VESCONTE MAGGIOLO

[*Portolan Atlas.*]
Naples, 1511.
Two single, eight double-page manuscript maps.

Vesconte Maggiolo was one of the most gifted cartographers of the sixteenth century. A Genoese, he worked in Naples from 1511 to 1518, when he returned to Genoa as official cartographer. He prepared this Atlas for an unknown noble family of Corsica. It was obtained by John Nicholas Brown in June 1893, the day after he had obtained the Agnese Atlas. It contains besides the standard portolan-style maps, an extraordinary world map important as an early depiction of the American discoveries.

The world map from our Maggiolo Atlas was made at Naples in 1511. It is one of the most important early maps of America to have survived. Maggiolo confronts certain geographical problems—he identifies North America with eastern Asia—but he avoids others, such as the connection between the northern and southern continents of America. His place names include "Lands found by Columbus," "Land of the English," "Land of the Corte Real and of the King of Portugal."

Color plate I.

JCB(3)1:52; JCBAR 13:19; JCB *Collection's Progress* 44; Wroth, *Verrazzano*, 43–44, 170–173, 292 (plate 12). Giuseppi Caraci, "A Little Known Atlas...," in *Imago Mundi*, II (1937), pp. 37–54; Giuseppi Caraci, "La produzione cartografica di Vesconte Maggiolo (1511–1549) ed il Nuovo Mondo," *Memorie Geografiche*, vol. IV, Rome, 1958, pp. 221–289.
Acquired 2 June 1893, Heredia Sale, Paris, by John Nicholas Brown, the donor.

102 GIOVANNI ANDREA DI VAVASSORE, FL. 1510-1572
Opera di Giovanni andrea Vavassore ditto Vadagnino.
[Venice, 1525?]
Woodcut map, 43 × 57 cm.

The date of execution of this extraordinary woodcut map is not clear. The map reflects geographical discoveries made before 1500, but none which were made afterward. A great deal of information, including over three hundred place names, is cramped onto its small surface. The names seem to be done in type. Did Vavassore not know American geography? or did he not care?—among the problems yet to be solved.

Plate XVI.

JCBAR 58:47-58; Leo Bagrow, *Giovanni Andreas di Vavassore*, Jenkintown, Pennsylvania, 1939, n. 11; Roberto Almagià, "Il Mappamundo di G. A. Vavassore," in *Rivista Geografica Italiana*, XXVII (1920). Acquired 1958. The gift of George H. Beans.

103 ANONYMOUS
M. D. XXXIIII. Del mese di Dicembre. La carta universale della terra firma & Isole delle Indie occidentali.
[Venice, ca. 1534.]
Woodcut map, 56 × 46 cm.

Because this map was included in *Summario de Historia de l'Indie Occidentali* (see number 31), a collection of writings edited by Giovanni Battista Ramusio, it is often called the "Ramusio map." It is derived from two navigational charts by Spanish royal pilots kept in the Casa de Contratación in Seville. This is the first printed map to portray the shape of South America, to convey the relationship of the Caribbean to the continents, and to show the continuous coast of North America. Only one other copy is known.

The originality of its contents is seen by comparing this map with others printed at Venice in the years just prior to it—the Bordone of 1528 (number 99), the Roselli in the year 1532 found in Bartolommeo da li Sonetti (number 98), and the Vavassore map (number 102). There is an immense jump from the tentative, inaccurate, and vague depictions of these printed maps to the fully developed, recognizably accurate Ramusio.

Plate XVII.

JCBAR 29:25-28; JCB *Collection's Progress* 75; Wroth, *Verrazzano*, pp. 201, 301, 318 (plate 39). Acquired 1926. Endowment funds.

104 BATTISTA AGNESE, FL. 1530-1564
[Manuscript Portolan Atlas of the World.]
[Venice, 1543-1545.]
Eleven maps on vellum, in ink, colors, and gold.

Battista Agnese was a Genoese mapmaker who worked in Venice in the mid-sixteenth century. He was a prolific producer of decorated manuscript maps; seventy-one surviving Agnese atlases were identified by

INDICVM MARE
C. DI BONA SPERANZA
AEGIPTVS
LIBIA INTERIOR
CIRCVLVS ARTICVS
TROPICVS CANCRI
AEQVINOCTIALIS
TROPICVS CAPRICORNI
CIRCVLVS ANTARTICVS
PERV
MVNDVS NOVVS
BRAZIL
CATAIO

II (cat. no. 104)   Battista Agnese. World Map. Venice, 1544. 29×22 cm. *Courtesy of Mr. and Mrs. Alfred J. Petteruti in memory of Anthony J. Petteruti, 1895–1973.*

Henry R. Wagner in his 1931 study. The decoration of the John Carter Brown copy is the most refined and beautiful of them all. This copy was made at the order of Charles V, the Holy Roman Emperor, to give to his son Philip, sixteen years old in 1543, who became King Philip II of Spain in 1556.

JCB(3)1:126; JCBAR 13:20; JCB *Collection's Progress* 45; H. R. Wagner, "The Manuscript Atlases of Battista Agnese, *The Papers of the Bibliographical Society of America*, vol. XXV (1931), pp. 1–110; *Imago Mundi*, IV (1947), pp. 28–30; Wroth, *Verrazzano*, pp. 188–191, 299 (plate 31); Jeannette D. Black, "Oval World Map by Battista Agnese," *A Portfolio Honoring Harold Hugo*, Meriden, Connecticut, 1978.
Acquired 1 June 1893, Spitzer Sale, Paris, by John Nicholas Brown, the donor.

Oval world map.
29 × 22 cm.

Agnese's world maps always showed the routes of Magellan (in black ink) and the Spanish silver fleet from America (in gold). The narrow body of land on the North American coast reflects Verrazzano's voyage along the coast of North Carolina, 1524–1525; the Florentine saw water beyond the Outer Banks and optimistically assumed that it was the Pacific Ocean. Some Agnese world maps of this period show a line across this "sea" to Asia indicating the "King of France's route to Cathay" (Verrazzano being in the service of France). Agnese diplomatically omitted the line and its explanation in the map prepared for the Spanish monarch.

Color plate II.

105 [MARCO FRANCESCO GISOLFO]
[Manuscript Portolan Atlas of the World.]
[Genoa? ca. 1565.]
Twelve double-page maps with four pages of signs and tables.
World map, 38 × 26 cm.

Marco Francesco Gisolfo of Genoa was a pupil of Battista Agnese and worked in his teacher's style. Only eight manuscripts attributed to Gisolfo are known, including three which were owned by members of the Medici family. The world map that we show is clearly derived from the Agnese type; comparison with reproductions of other copies reveals that only details of the decorative elements vary in Gisolfo's manuscripts.

JCBAR 13:20; Seymour de Ricci, *Census of Medieval and Renaissance Manuscripts in the United States*, New York, 1935–1940, JCB 12; Justin Winsor, "Battista Agnese and American Cartography in the Sixteenth Century," *Proceedings of the Massachusetts Historical Society*, 2d ser., vol. II, Boston, May 1897, pp. 372–385.
Acquired 1885 by John Nicholas Brown, the donor.

106 ANONYMOUS
"Florentine Goldsmith's Map."
[Italy, 1544?]
Engraved world map, 24×21 cm.

This is a mysterious world map—its title is a Library tradition, a handle given to it by F. S. Ellis, the bookseller who sold it to Sophia Augusta Brown, John Carter Brown's widow. There is a closely related manuscript copy dated 1552 in a portolan atlas by Giorgio Calapoda. However, Calapoda may well have copied this engraving, as the other maps known to be by him do not resemble the style of the world map. At any rate, the engraving is a much finer piece of art. A highlight of the map is the isthmus of North Carolina which Verrazzano had first reported. Lower California appears as a peninsula (its first appearance on a dated map was 1542), but the Amazon, which first appeared on dated maps in 1546, is not shown here.

Plate XVIII.

Wroth, *Verrazzano*, pp. 194–195, 299, 318 (plate 33); Theodore Layng, *Sixteenth-Century Maps Relating to Canada*, Ottawa, 1956, no. 359; Adolf Erik Nordenskiöld, *Periplus: An Essay on the Early History of Charts and Sailing Directions* . . . , Stockholm, 1897, pp. 65–66, 159a (plates 25 and 26).
Acquired 1884 by Sophia Augusta Brown.

107 GIACOMO GASTALDI, FL. 1500–1565
Universale.
1546. Giacomo Cosmographo in Venetia.
Engraved world map, 54×33 cm.

This is a proof copy of the first state of Giacomo Gastaldi's first world map, described as "one of the most important maps of the sixteenth century." In it North America is shown connected to Asia by a broad body of land that begins about where California would be. California is shown as a peninsula and the seven cities of Coronado appear.

Plate XXII.

Tooley 5; Wroth, *Verrazzano*, pp. 201–203, 301–302, 318 (plate 40); *World Encompassed* 121 (plate 36).
Acquired 1890 by John Nicholas Brown, the donor.

George H. Beans of Philadelphia collected sixteenth-century maps of America engraved by Italians at a time when they were not as well appreciated or understood as they are now. His sponsorship of "Tall Tree Publications," monographic studies of maps in his Collection, helped advance our appreciation and understanding of early engraved maps. Beginning in 1956 and continuing through 1961 he donated his Collection to the John Carter Brown Library in one of the most extensive gifts ever given to the Library. After years of disabling illness, Mr. Beans died in December 1978. We commemorate Mr. Beans's scholarship and his generosity, and we honor the memory of a man who honored the Library by entrusting his Collection to its care.

108 GIACOMO GASTALDI, FL. 1500–1565
La Universale Descrittione Del Mondo. . . .
Venetia, per Matthio Pagano . . . M.LXII [sic; i.e., 1562].

In 1562, Gastaldi published a large map of the whole world and brought out this small book to describe the map. No presently known map can be surely identified as the one Gastaldi describes, although various maps have been offered as candidates. In the section of *La Universale Descrittione del Mondo* treating Asia the author describes, as if a known fact, a water passage on the northeastern boundary of the continent separating it from America, which he called "Streto di Anian." The strait now named for Vitus Bering was not "discovered" until 1728, and it is hard to know how Gastaldi had deduced its existence nearly two centuries previously. This unique copy of *La Universale Descrittione del Mondo* is one of the monuments of early cartographical literature and is an intriguing glimpse into some of the thoughts of a great cartographer at work.

Plate XI.

JCBAR 57:27–30; JCB *Collection's Progress* 106 (illustration number XXII); Wroth, *Verrazzano*, p. 203.
Acquired 1957. The gift of George H. Beans.

109 GIACOMO GASTALDI, FL. 1500–1565
Universale Descrittione Di Tutta La Terra Conosciuta Fin Qui.
Venice, [1565].
Engraved world map, 57×44 cm.

For twenty-three years following the 1546 *Universale*, Gastaldi was the leading mapmaker of Italy in regard both to his technical execution and the information he assembled and interpreted. The Beans gift includes numerous versions of Gastaldi's world maps. These illustrate the problem faced by a cartographer: he must reconcile information from many sources, often vague or contradictory, even merely verbal, to produce an uncompromising interpretation, a single bold and definite line. In this map an enormous continent with Hippopotomi, Elephants, Griffins has emerged. The vast Antarctica was to remain until proven a myth by Captain James Cook two centuries later.

World Encompassed 123; Tooley 11.
Acquired 1857. The gift of George H. Beans.

110 [GIACOMO GASTALDI], FL. 1500–1565
Totius Orbis Descriptio.
[Venice, 1562–1569.]
Engraved world map, 78×49 cm.

In this world map Gastaldi returns to the concept of the Straits of Anian—the narrow body of water between northern America and Asia—which he had proposed in his "lost" map of 1562. Florida is represented as a bulbous oval attached by a narrow neck; the representation of the east coast of North America lacks the accuracy and artistic sharpness of his *Universale Descrittione*. In the four corners are views of Venice, Rome, Naples, and Genoa.

Plate XXIII.

Tooley 22.
Acquired 1957. The gift of George H. Beans.

111 GIANFRANCESCO CAMOCIO, AFTER GIACOMO GASTALDI
Cosmographia Universalis.
Venice, Camocio, 1569.
Engraved world map in four sheets, 105 × 63 cm.

This world map derives from a map, now perhaps lost, prepared by Gastaldi as the culmination of his thirty years of interpreting the shape of the world. Several Gastaldi maps, much larger than this one, have been offered as the original from which this one was copied, but each failed at some point to correspond with Gastaldi's own description of what he intended to do.

JCBAR 57:25–30; JCB *Collection's Progress* 181; Tooley 20; *World Encompassed* 125 (plate XXXVII); George H. Beans, *A Large World Map . . . by Joan Franciscus Camotius*, Jenkintown, Pennsylvania, 1933.
Acquired 1958. The gift of George H. Beans.

112 MICHELE TRAMEZINO, FL. 1539–1582
[*The World in hemispheres*. Engraved by Giulio de' Musi.]
Venice, 1554.
Copperplate engravings, four sheets pasted in two, 75 × 75 cm. each.

These two hemispheres use "Bacon's Meridian Projection" to resolve the problem of portraying a sphere on a flat surface. Roger Bacon devised the projection three centuries before enough of the world was known to need it. A notable feature of this map is the wide sea separating northern Asia from northern America.

Plates XXV and XXVI.

JCBAR 57:22–23; JCB *Collection's Progress* 56; *World Encompassed* 124 (plate XXXV); Tooley 18.
Acquired 1956. The gift of George H. Beans.

113 OLAUS MAGNUS, ARCHIBISHOP OF UPSALA, 1490–1557
[*Carta Marina et descriptio septentrionelium terrarum.*]
Romae ex Typis Antonii Lafreri Seguani Anno MDLXXII [1572].
Engraved map in two sheets joined, 84 × 55 cm.

Information about Norse voyages to the western North Atlantic was available in Italy early in the sixteenth century. Antonio Lafreri, the best Roman cartographer, engraved this map which had first been published

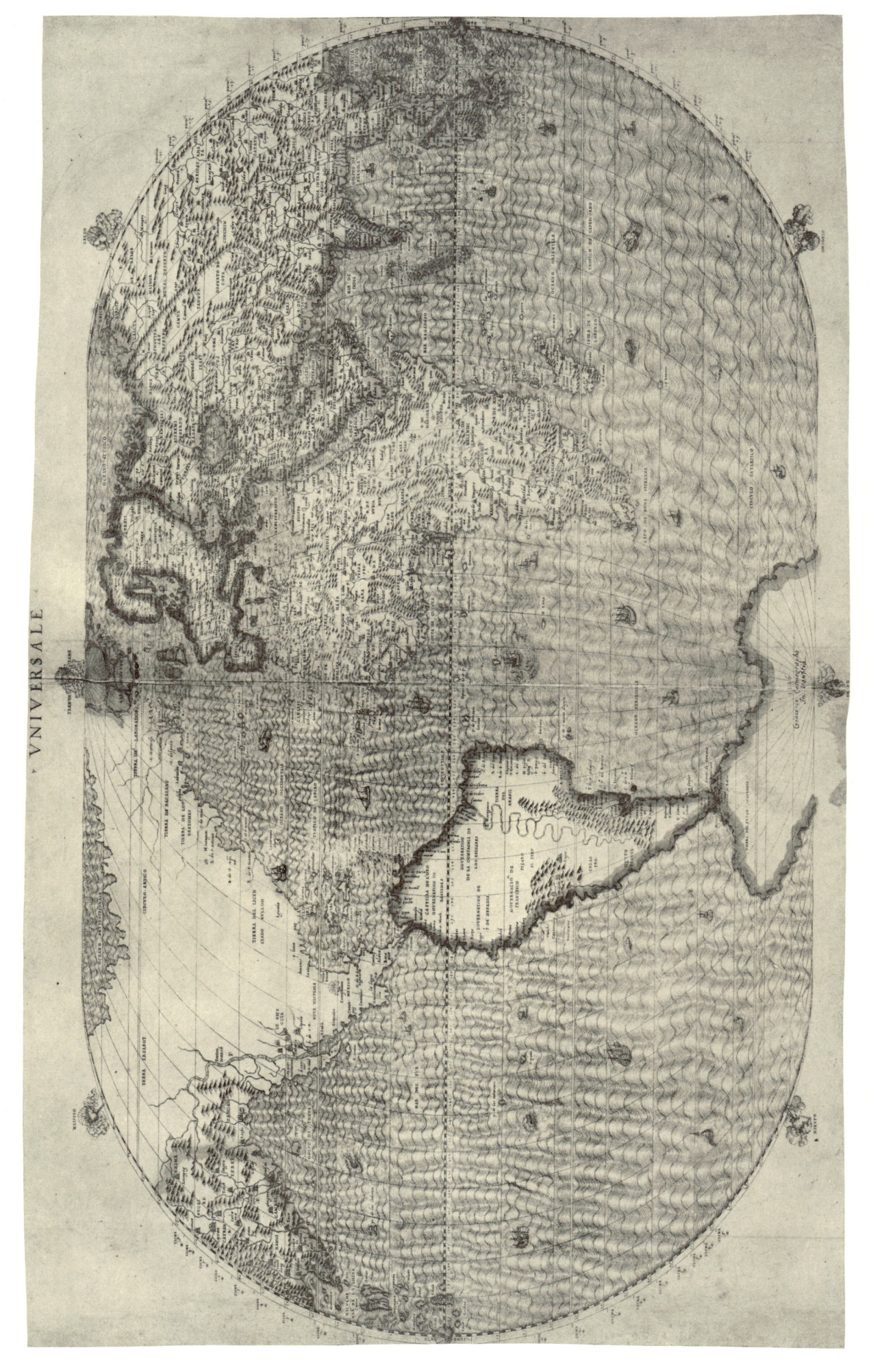

XXII (cat. no. 107) Gastaldi. *Universale.* Venice, 1546. 54×33 cm. *Courtesy of The Rhode Island Hospital Trust National Bank.*

XXIII (cat. no. 110) Gastaldi. *Totius Orbis Descriptio.* [Venice, 1562–1569.] 54×33 cm.

XXIV (cat. no. 113) Olaus. Norse voyages. Rome, 1572. 84×55 cm.

XXV (cat. no. 112) Tramezino. New World. Venice, 1554. 75×75 cm.

XXVI (cat. no. 112)   Tramezino. Old World. Venice, 1554. 75×75 cm.

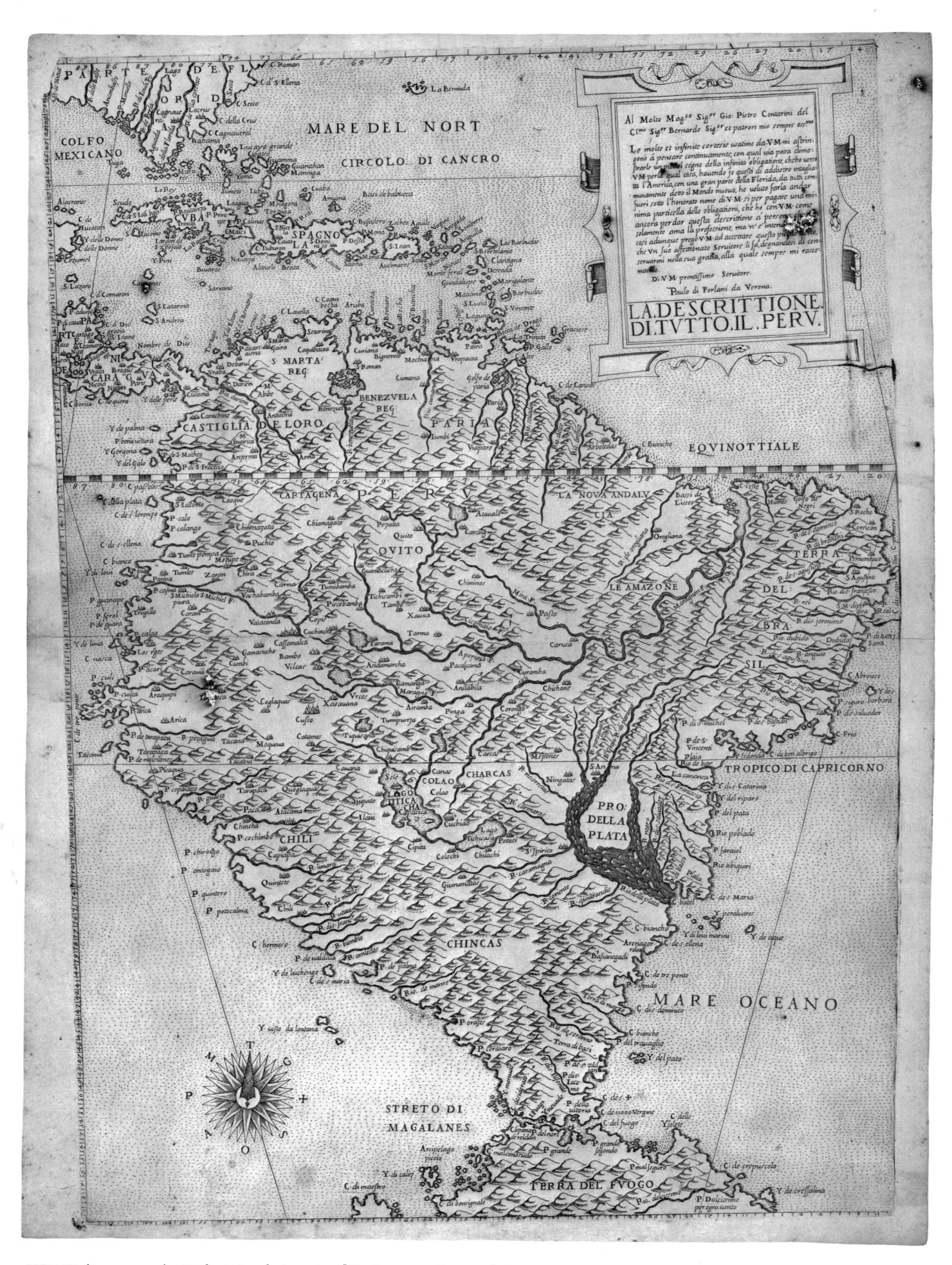

XXVII (cat. no. 115)   Forlani. South America. [Venice, ca. 1564–1572.] 67 × 53 cm.

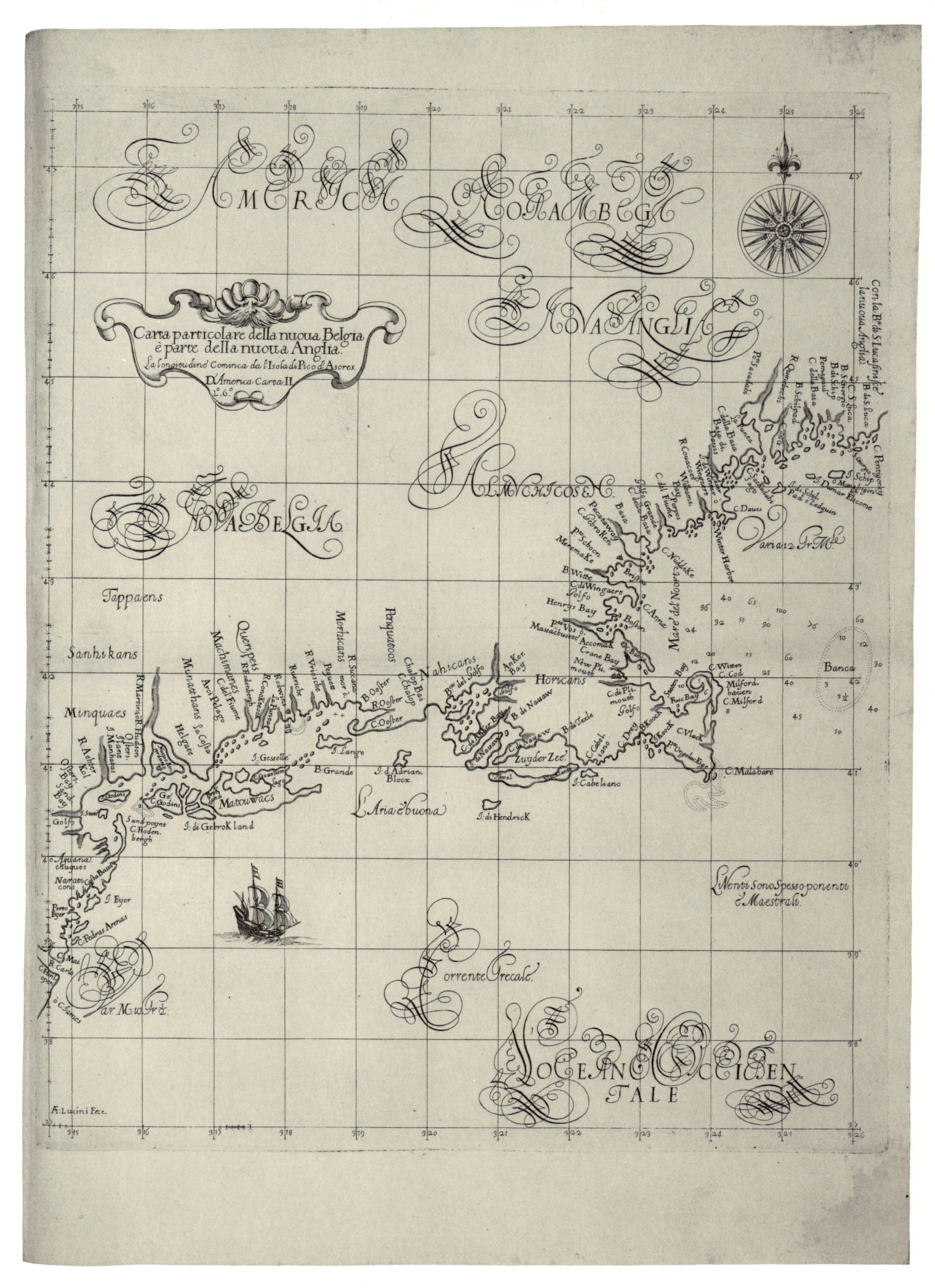

XXVIII (cat. no. 125)   Dudley. Map of New England. Florence, 1661. 30×40 cm.

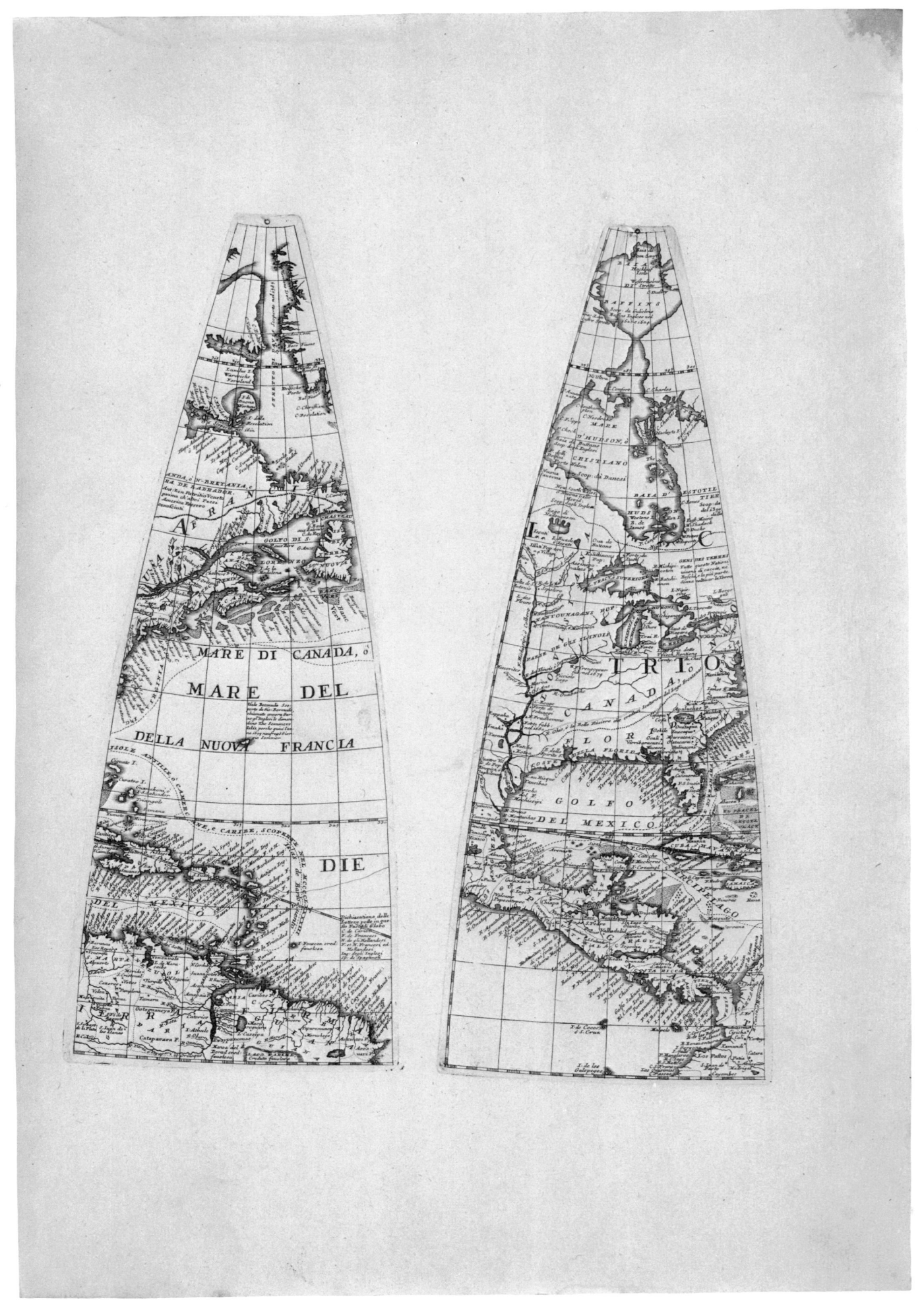

XXIX (cat. no. 126)   Coronelli. Gore of New England. Venice, 1705. 40×20 cm.

at Venice as a woodcut in 1539. It shows that Scandinavian knowledge of the western North Atlantic had receded and was inferior to what was commonly available on Italian maps of that time.

Plate XXIV.

JCBAR 60:31–32, 49; 65:26; Tooley 44; Edward Lyman, *The Carta Marina of Olaus Magnus*, Jenkintown, Pennsylvania, 1949, pp. 27–35; *World Encompassed* 151 (plate XLIII the Beans copy).
Acquired 1960. The gift of George H. Beans.

114 ANTONIO FLORIAN, FL. 1545–1560

[World in gores, northern and southern hemispheres.]
[Venice, 1556.]
Engraved map in two sheets, 43 × 47.5 cm. each.

How do you portray the globe on a flat map? That is the problem all cartographers have to confront. Florian prepared gores which could be cut out and attached to a globe, or preserved flat as in our copy, minimizing distortion. Other cartographers used other techniques such as the cordiform maps (see numbers 119 and 121).

Plates XIX and XX.

Tooley 23; Rodolfo Gallo, "Antonio Florian and His Mappe Monde," in *Imago Mundi*, VI (1950), pp. 35–38.
Acquired 1957. The gift of George H. Beans.

115 PAOLO FORLANI, FL. 1558–1574

La Descrittione Di Tutto Il Peru.
[Venice, ca. 1564–1572.]
Engraved map of South America, 51 × 36 cm.

This is the first map which purports to show the interior of South America in great detail. The bulging shape of the continent, the mountain ranges liberally sprinkled over the entire area, the enlarged Río de la Plata, the fanciful lakes, and wildly misplaced cities (Quito appears here just north of the center of the continent) indicate that Forlani did not have as much information as the abundance of detail suggests he had. The mapmaker had always to balance between presenting what he knew for sure and what was probable, or possible. Forlani filled his map with interesting possibilities.

Plate XXVII.

JCBAR 59:37–39; Tooley 93.
Acquired 1957. The gift of George H. Beans.

116 PAOLO FORLANI, FL. 1558–1574
. . . un disegno, overo una particolar descrittione di tutte le navigationi del Mondo nuovo. . . .
Di Venetia a di xiiii Decembre M.D.LXXiiii [1574]. A presso Simon Pinargenti.
Engraved map in two sheets joined, 67×53 cm.

In this map of the "New World," Forlani includes all the globe discovered since Columbus from the Canary Islands westward to Asia. The depiction of South America carries over the detailed information included in his earlier map. His interpretation of North America is ambitious in the detail it offers. The width of the continent is enormous, with the eastern coast extended easterly in a way that doubles the land mass. The Straits of Anian appear with convincing detail. Lower California appears as accurately as could be expected, but Florida is a nub of a projection from the mainland.

Shortly after its publication this map was used as copy for one of the magnificent mural maps in the Caprarola palace, the summer residence of Cardinal Alessandro Farnese.

JCBAR 59:37–39; JCB *Collection's Progress* 177 (plate XXXI); Tooley 82; George Kish, "The 'Mural Atlas' of Caprarola," in *Imago Mundi*, X (1953), pp. 51–55.
Acquired 1958. The gift of George H. Beans.

117 BOLOGNINO ZALTIERI, FL. 1566–1570
Il Disegno del discoperto della nova Francia.
[Venice, 1566.]
Engraved map, 40.5×27 cm.

This is an undated early state of a map of North America formerly believed to be the first representation of the Straits of Anian. Priority of showing the Straits must now be given to Gastaldi's map of 1562. Certain other features, such as the bulbous Florida, suggest it was derived from Gastaldi's much more detailed *Totius Orbis Descriptio*. This map reflects Spanish explorations of the Southwest of North America during the 1540's. The term *Sierra Nevada* appears near the Straits of Anian, and Coronado's elusive Quivira not far to the south.

JCBAR 57:28–30; *World Encompassed* 207; L. C. Wroth, *Early Cartography of the Pacific*, New York, 1944, p. 251, no. 51 (plate XI); Fite and Freeman 21; Wagner (N.W.) 69.
Acquired 1915. Endowment funds.

118A [NICOLAS DE NICOLAY, SIEUR D'ARFEUILLE], 1517–1583
Navigationi del mondo novo.
Venice, Giovanni Francesco Camocio, 1560.
Engraved map, 24×36.5 cm.

118B [NICOLAS DE NICOLAY, SIEUR D'ARFEUILLE], 1517–1583
Printed by Ferrando Bertelli. Venice, ca. 1565.
Engraved map, 24.5×36 cm.

Two versions of the same map by different Venetian map publishers illustrate how the same basic information can be used in different ways. They are both a slightly reduced, revised version of Nicolay's "Nouveau

Monde," first published in Pedro de Medina, *L'Art de Naviguer*, Lyon, 1554. It is basically a map of the Atlantic with portions of eastern North America, northern South America, northwestern Africa, and western Europe included. The Bertelli version is more concerned with details of the interior than that of Camocio, and shows fanciful interior mountains and cities not on the earlier version. The Amazon is treated differently in each and Bertelli includes a lake in New France. The Library also has the Camocio version dated 1563.

Tooley 77 and 78.
The Bertelli version acquired 1957 as a gift of George H. Beans.
The Camocio version acquired 1968. Associates of the John Carter Brown Library.

119 ORONCE FINÉ, 1494–1555

Cosmographia Universalis ab Orontio olim descripta.
[Venice], Joannes Paulus Cimerlinus Veronensis in aes incidebat Anno 1566.
Engraved map, 59×51.5 cm.

Oronce Finé, a French mathematician, offered the cordiform—heart-shaped—map as a solution to the problem of portraying a globe in two dimensions. His solution as adapted by Giovanni Paolo Cimerlino is handsome and has merit—it is still occasionally used.

Plate XXI.

JCBAR 60:32–33, 49; Tooley 19; *World Encompassed* 153 (plate XXXIV).
Acquired 1960. The gift of George H. Beans.

120 [NICCOLÒ ZENO], 1515–1565

Frisland.
[Venice, ca. 1570.]
Engraved map, 19×24.5 cm.

Venice contributed a pair of brothers to the contenders for visitors to North America before Columbus. Antonio and Niccolò Zeno were supposed to have sailed westward across the North Atlantic in 1380 or '90 and to have been shipwrecked on "Frisland" where they were purported to have lived for some years. They returned to Venice, and their documents remained in the family until a descendant published them, including a smaller version of this map, in 1558. The story has been the subject of a controversy for the past four hundred years.

Tooley 222; see *World Encompassed* 76 (on woodcut version in the book).
Acquired 1960. The gift of George H. Beans.

121 [HADJI AHMAD]

[The representation of the whole world, depicted in its entirety.]
[Venice, 1568.]

Hadji Ahmad, a Tunisian slave, drew this cordiform map in 1559/60 with extensive commentary in the Persian language using Arabic characters. A printer, Marcantonio Giustiniano, had woodblocks prepared and in 1568 had apparently run off prints from the blocks to sell in the East when the government suppressed the project and seized the woodcuts.

In 1795 Christoforo Antonio Loredan, superintendent of the criminal archives of the Council of Ten, found the blocks in drawers where they had been put and forgotten. Thinking they were hieroglyphs, Loredan had the state printer, Pinelli, make an impression. Only when the pieces were put together did they realize that they made a map. An orientalist, the Abbé Simeone Assemoni, was engaged to add modern commentary. Twenty-four impressions were made from the blocks by Pinelli; the Library's copy is one of those twenty-four (and one of six known survivors). The blocks themselves still survive in the library of San Marco in Venice, but as they have been split for many years, no more copies may be printed from them.

JCBAR 65:26–27; JCB *Collection's Progress* 57.
Acquired 1962. Associates of the John Carter Brown Library.

122 [ELIA ENDASIAN]
[America, according to recent authorities.]
[Venice], 1787.
Engraved map, colored, 46.3 × 63.1 cm.

There is little known about the knowledge of America in eighteenth-century Armenia. In 1963 the Library obtained an Armenian translation of William Robertson's *History of America* (Vispasanouthian Amerikoy . . .) printed at Trieste, 1784–1786 originally published at London in 1777. The Armenian text was translated by Dr. Minas Gasparian from Italian, the first edition of which appeared at Florence in 1777.

It was in Italy, too, that this map of America with Armenian lettering was printed. Although the information contained on the map derived from standard maps, it is noteworthy that Venice served as the source of standard information about the West to the East two hundred years after the appearance of the Hadji Ahmed map.

Acquired 1974. Associates of the John Carter Brown Library.

123 ARNOLDO DI ARNOLDI, D. 1602
Universale Descrittione del Mondo.
[Siena, 1601.]
Engraved map in two sheets joined, 80.5 × 51 cm.

Arnoldi was a Belgian who lived in Bologna from 1595 to 1600 and worked there for the geographer and astronomer Giovanni Antonio Magini. In 1600 he moved to Siena where he died in 1602. The two Sienese years were fruitful ones as he produced a large world map of which this is a reduced copy.

Roberto Almagia, *Il Planisfero di Arnoldo di Arnoldi (1600)*, Rome, 1934.
Acquired 1962. Associates of the John Carter Brown Library.

124 ARNOLDO DI ARNOLDI, D. 1602

[Maps of America, Africa, Europe, and Asia.]

Siena, 1601.

Engraved map of America, 48.5 × 37 cm.

Arnoldi's maps are based on ones prepared by Abraham Ortelius, the great Dutch mapmaker whose work from 1570/1 was eclipsing Italian cartographical efforts. Arnoldi added to Ortelius information—such as the Roanoke settlements—derived from later sources. This series of maps contains the coat of arms of Scipione Bargaglia, and the European map contains a dedication to the patron who made publication of the four maps possible.

JCBAR 58:56–59; Roberto Almagiá, *Monumenta Cartographia Vaticana*, Vatican, 1944–1945, vol. II, p. 72; George H. Beans, "Some Notes from the Tall Tree Library," in *Imago Mundi*, VI (1949), p. 33.
Acquired 1958. The gift of George H. Beans.

125 SIR ROBERT DUDLEY, STYLED DUKE OF NORTHUMBERLAND AND EARL OF WARWICK, 1574–1649

Arcano Dell' Mare Di D. Ruberto Dudleo Duca Di Nortumbria E Conte Di Warvich. . . .

In Fiorenza, M.DC.LXI [1661]. Nella Nuova Stamperia Per Giuseppe Cocchini.

Sir Robert Dudley was the son of Queen Elizabeth's lover, the Earl of Leicester. In 1605 he left England, his family, and all his possessions, to settle in Florence, where he served as engineer to the Grand Duke of Tuscany. It was he who drained the swamps below Pisa and developed Leghorn into a fortified port. He designed ships and war machines to serve the Grand Duke's military projects, and he collected maps and plans of machines. These collections, along with his own writings, were printed first in 1646 and, more amply, in 1661. The high quality of Florentine engraving is displayed in the double-page map of the Gulf of Mexico—an area to which Dudley sailed as a youthful English pirate in 1595. The engraver for the entire book was Antonio Francesco Lucini who was born in Florence about 1610, a pupil of Jacques Callot and a friend of Stefano della Bella. Lucini worked for twelve years in a Tuscan village, using five thousand pounds of copper in preparing the engravings for this work.

Plate XXVIII.

JCB(3)3:53–55; *World Encompassed* 191.
Acquired 1906. Endowment funds.

126 VINCENZO CORONELLI, 1650–1718

Palestra Litteraria, O Invito Dell' Accademia Cosmografica a suoi Argonauti. . . .

Gli Argonauti In Venetia [1705].

Vincenzo Coronelli was a Franciscan (he became General of the order in 1701), a skilled cartographer, and a man of great energies. He was cosmographer to the Republic of Venice, founded the first geographical society, Accademia Cosmografica degli Argonauti, and turned the Venetian Convento de Frari where he lived into an active publishing house for maps and engravings. The book exhibited here, usually known as *Libro de Globi*, is a collection of engraved sections for globes, called gores, which, if assembled, would comprise two globes, one of the earth and another of the heavens. Copies of the book were issued in different forms as they were intended to be cut up and used as globes. That they were so used is indicated by the fact that there are a good number of Coronelli globes which have survived, but relatively few copies of the gores in book form.

Plate XXIX.

Helen Wallis, "Introduction" to Vincenzo Coronelli, *Libro dei Globi*, Amsterdam, Theatrum Orbis Terrarum, 1969 (facsimile publication); Mario Witt, "Introduction" to Vincenzo Coronelli, *Ships and Other Sorts of Craft Used by the Various Nations of the World, Venice, 1690*, London [1970].
Acquired 1913. Endowment funds.

127 VINCENZO SCOTTI
Tavola delle più esatte ed usitate Bandiere che si alberano.
Livorno, 1796.
Flag sheet, 49 × 39 cm.

Of the 110 flags displayed on this table seven are those of the United States. The *Tavola* is a reminder of the commerce enjoyed by Providence merchants with Italy after the American Revolution. It came to the Library from the estate of Senator Theodore Francis Green, a descendant of Welcome Arnold, a Providence merchant who sent ships to trade at Livorno in the 1790's.

Endpapers.

Acquired 1969.

INDEX

Numbers refer to entry in Catalogue. Subject entries are marked with an asterisk.

Achenwall, Gottfried, *Précis de l'état* (1771) 77
Adams, John, President, *Defence of the Constitution* (1787) 90
Agnese, Battista, [*Manuscript portolan atlas*] (1543–1545) 104
Albenino, Nicolao de, *Verdadera relacion* (1549) 27
Albergati, Vianesio, *La Pazzia* (1541) (1543) 24
Alfieri, Vittorio, *L'America libera* (1784) 91
———, *L'America libera* (1805) 93
———, *La Guerra in America* (ca. 1784) 92
Anghiera, Pietro Martire d', *Libretto* (1504) 9
———, *Opera* (1511) 30
Antonio de Olave, *Passio gloriosi martyris* (1532) 34
Arnoldi, Arnoldo de, [*Maps of America, Africa, Europe, and Asia*] (1601) 124
———, *Universale descrittione del mondo* (1601) 123
Avisi Particolari delle Indie (1552) 36

Badia, Marc'Antonio, *Compendio della guerra* (1763) 74
Bado, Sebastiano, *Anastasis corticis peruviae* (1663) 51
Bartolommeo da li Sonetti, *Isolario* (1532) 98
Beccaria, Cesare, Marchese, *An essay on crimes and punishments* (1778) 88
Bellin, Jacques Nicolas, *Descrizione geografica* (1758) 73
Benzoni, Girolamo, *La Historia del Mondo Nuovo* (1565) 28
Bertelli, Fernando, *Navigationi del mondo novo* (ca. 1565) 118
Blackford, Dominique, *see* Achenwall
Bordone, Benedetto, *Libro . . . da tutte l'isole del mondo* (1528) 99
Botta, Carlo, *Storia della Guerra dell'Independenza* (1809) 97
Boturini Beneducci, Lorenzo, *Idea de una nueva historia* (1746) 65

Bressani, Francesco Giuseppe, *Breve relatione . . . nella Nuova Francia* (1653) 54

Cà da Mosto, Alvise da, *Itineribus* (1515) 2
Camocio, Giacomo, *Cosmographia Universalis* (1569) 111
———, *Navigationi del mondo novo* (1560) 118
Capitulo over recetta delo . . . Guaiana (1520) 49
Carletti, Francesco, *Ragionamenti* (1701) 57
Carli, Diogini, *Viaggio* (1671) 56
Carli, Giovanni Rinaldo, *Delle lettere Americane* (1780) 94
Carta universale (Ramusio) (ca. 1534) 103
Cartari, Vicenzo, *Imagini de gli dei* (1626) 63
Castiglioni, Luigi, *Viaggio negli Stati Uniti* (1790) 96
Clavijero, Francisco Javier, *Storia Antica del Messico* (1780) 71
Colombo, Cristoforo, *Epistola* (1493) 6
———, *De Insulis inventis* (1494) 7
———, *Eyn Schön hubsch lesen* (1497) 8
———, [*Manuscript Capitulations*] ([1504]) 10
*Colon, Fernando, *Historie* (1571) 39
*Gambara, Lorenzo, *De Navigatione Christophori Columbi* (1581) 42
*Giorgini Giovanni, *Il Mondo Nuovo* (1596) 44
*Giovio, Paolo, *Elogia virorum bellica* (1551) 40
*———, *Elogia virorum bellica* (1571) 41
*Maffei, Raffaele, *Commentariorum Urbanorum* (1506) 37
*Montalboddo, Francanzano da, *Paesi novamente retrovati* (1507) 29
Psalterum Hebreum, Grecum, Arabicum (1516) 38
*Stella, Giulio Cesare, *Columbeidos priores duo* (1590) 43
*Stigliani, Tomaso, *Del mondo nuovo* (1617) 45
Colón, Fernando, *Historie* (1571) 39
Coronelli, Vincenzo, *Palestra litteraria* (1705) 126

[81]

Dudley, Sir Robert, *Arcano dell'mare* (1661) 125

Eandi, Giuseppe, *Memorie Istoriche intorno . . . Giambatista Beccaria* (1783) 82
Endasian, Elia, [*America, Armenian map*] (1787) 122

Finé, Oronce, *Cosmographia universalis* (1566) 119
"Florentine Goldsmith's Map" (1544?) 106
Florian, Antonio, [*World in gores*] (1556) 114
Forlani, Paolo, *Un disegno* (1574) 116
———, *La Descrittione di tutto il Peru* (1564–1572) 115
Fracastoro, Girolamo, *Syphilis* (1530) 50
Franklin, Benjamin, *Avviso a quegli* (1785) 86
———, *Il buon huomo Ricciardo* (1797) 87
———, *Descrizione della stufa* (1788) 85
———, *Opere politiche* (1783) 84
———, *Rules for reducing a great empire* (1793) 89
———, *Scelta di lettere* (1774) 83
  *[Achenwall, Gottfried], *Précis de l'état* (1771) 77
  *Eandi, Giuseppe, *Memorie istoriche* (1783) 82

Gambara, Lorenzo, *De navigationi* (1581) 42
Garcés, Julian, *De habilitate* (1537) 23
Gastaldi Giacomo, *Totius orbis* (1562–1569) 110
———, *Cosmographia universale* (1569) 111
———, *Universale* (1546) 107
———, *La universale descrittione* (1562) 108
——— *Universale descrittione* (1565) 109
Il Gazzettiere Americano (1763) 81
Gemelli Careri, Giovanni Francesco, *Giro del mondo* (1719) 62
Geminiani, Francesco, *An abstract of the art of playing violin* (1769) 68
Genovesi, Antonio, *Lezioni di commercio* (1769) 76
Gilii, Filippo Salvatore, *Saggio di storia Americana* (1780) 72
Gisolfo, Marco Francesco, [*Manuscript portolan atlas*] (ca. 1565) 105
Gualterotti, Raffaelo, *L'America* (1611) 47

Hadji Ahmad, [*The whole world*] (1568) 121
Hennepin, Louis, *Descrizione della Luigiana* (1686) 60

———, Zani, Valerio, *Il genio vagante* (1691–1693) 61
Houssaye, Abraham Nicolas Amelot de la, *La storia del governo di Venezia* (1681) 58

Isolano, Isidoro, *In hoc volumine* (1517) 22

Jesuits. *Avisi particolari* (1552) 36
———. *Lettres edifiantes* (Kino map) (1705) 53
  *Bressani, Francesco Giuseppe, *Breve relatione* (1653) 54
  *Clavijero, Francisco Javier, *Storia antica del Messico* (1780) 71
  *Gilii, Filippo Salvadore, *Saggio* (1780) 72
  *Jolis, Joseph, *Saggio* (1789) 70
Jolis, Joseph, *Saggio sulla storia naturale del Gran Chaco* (1789) 70

Kino, Eusebio Francisco, *Passage par terre* (1705) 53
Knox, William, *Stato presente della nazione* (1775) 80

Lafreri, Antonio, *Carta marina* (1572) 113
Lilio, Zacharias, *De origine* (1496) 18

Maffei, Raffaele, *Commentariorum urbanorum* (1506) 37
*Magellan, Ferdinand, see Pigafetta
Maggiolo, Vesconte, [*Portolan atlas*] (1511) 101
Magnus, Olaus, *Carta marina* (1572) 113
*Martin de Valencia, see Antonio de Olave
Martinelli, Vincenzo, *Istoria del governo d'Inghilterra e delle sue colonie* (1776) 78
Mazzei, Filippo, *Recherches historiques* (1788) 95
*Medici family, see Vespucci (no. 11); Mellini; Gualterotti
Mellini, Domenico, *Descrizione della entrata* (1566) 25
Montalboddo, Francanzano da, *Paesi novamenta retrovati* (1507) 29
Moscardo, Lodovico, *Note overo memorie* (1656) 64

Nicolay, Nicolas, *Navigationi* (1560) 118

Ovalle, Alonso de, *Historica relacion* (1646) 55

Pasqualigo, Pietro, *Ad Hemanvelem Lusitaniae* (1501) 20
Paul III, Pope, *see* Garcés
Piccolomini, Aenaeus Silvius, *Cosmographia* (1509) 4
Pico della Mirandola, Giovanni Francesco, *De rerum praenotione* (1507) 21
Pigafetta, Antonio, *Le voyage* (1525) 26
Pius II, Pope, *see* Piccolomini
*Pizarro, Francisco, *see* Xerez
*Pizarro, Gonzalo, *see* Albenino
Polo, Marco, *In cui si tratta le meravigliose cose* (1555) 1
Ponza, Giorgio, *La science de l'homme de qualité* (1684) 59
Porcacchi da Castiglione, *L'Isole piu famose del mondo* (1572) 100
Possevino, Antonio, *Apparato all'historia* (1598) 33
Psalterum, Hebreum, Grecum (1516) 38
Ptolemaeus, Claudius, *Cosmographia* (1477) 3
———, [*Atlas of 15 maps*] (ca. 1440) 5
———, *Geographia* (1507) 19

Ramusio, Giovanni Battista, *Carta universale* (ca. 1534) 103
———, *Summario de la generale historia* (1534) 31
———, *Terza volume delle navigationi* (1556) 32
Raynal, Guillaume Thomas François, *Storia dell'America* (1778) 79
Ruysch, Johannes, [*World map*] *in* Ptolemy, *Geographia* (1507) 19

Sangro, *see* Sansevero
Sansevero, Raimondo di Sangro, Principe de, *Lettera apologetica* (1750) 66
Scotti, Vincenzo, *Tavola delle . . . Bandiere* (1796) 127
Smeducci, Girolamo Bartolomméi, *L'America poema eroico* (1650) 48
Stampiglia, Silvio, *La Partenope fiesta* (ca. 1760) 67
Stigliani, Tomaso, *Del mondo nuovo* (1617) 45

La storia dell'anno MDCCLXIX (1770) 75
Strozzi, Giovanni Battista, [*Manuscript poem on Vespucci*] (before 1601) 46
Suárez de Figueroa, Miguel, *Templo de . . . San Francisco . . . de el Peru* (1675) 69

Torti, Francesco, *Therapeutice specialis ad febres* (1712) 52
Tramezino, Michele, [*The world in hemispheres*] (1554) 112

Vavassore, Giovanni Andrea di, *Opera* (1525?) 102
*Verrazzano, Giovanni da, *see* Ramusio, *Terzo volume*
Vespucci, Amerigo, *Albericus Vespuccius laurentio* (1503) 11
———, *Mundus novus* (1504) 12–14
———, *Von der neü gefunden Region* (1505) 15
———, *Van der nieuwer werelt* (1508) 16
  *Anghiera, Pietro Martire d', *Opera* (1511) 30
  *Gualterotti, Raffaelo, *L'America* (1611) 46
  *Montalboddo, Francanzano da, *Paesi novamente retrovati* (1507) 29
  *Smeducci, Girolamo, *L'America poema eroico* (1650) 4
  *Strozzi, Giovanni Battista, [*Manuscript poem on Vespucci*] (before 1601) 46
  *Waldseemüller, Martin, *Cosmographiae introductio* (1507) 17

Waldseemüller, Martin, *Cosmographiae introductio* (1507) 17

Xerez, Francisco de, *Libro primo de la conquista* (1535) 35

Zaltieri, Bolognino, *Il disegno del discoperto* (1566) 117
Zani, Conte Valerio, *Il genio vagante* (1691–1693) 61
Zeno, Niccolò, *Frisland* (ca. 1570) 120

Design, composition, letterpress printing, and binding by
THE STINEHOUR PRESS

Halftone photography and offset printing by
THE MERIDEN GRAVURE COMPANY

Toscana
Imperatore
Francia
Spagna
Portogallo
Napoli
Sardegna
Prussia
Olanda
Venezia
Anburgo
Brabant
Weiman
Lubecca
Rostoc
Gerusalemme
Monaco
Modena
Lucca
Massa e Carrara
Corsica
Porta
Tripoli
Tunis

Toscana
Bandiera di Guerra, e sua Fiamma

Francia
1. Bandiera Bianca di Guerra, e Mercantile, e sua Fiamma
2. Detta della Squadra Blu, e sua Fiamma

10. Band. Particolare di Dong.
11. Detta C. I. di Calais
Inghilterra